CROSSROADS 1

Oxford University Press
200 Madison Avenue
New York, NY 10016 USA

Walton Street
Oxford OX2 6DP England

OXFORD is a trademark of Oxford University Press.

Library of Congress Cataloging-in-Publication Data

Frankel, Irene
        Crossroads 1 Student Book/by Irene Frankel and Cliff Meyers, with
Earl W. Stevick.

        1. English language—Textbooks for foreign speakers. I. Meyers,
Cliff. II. Stevick, Earl W. III. Title.
PE1128.F6745 1991   428.2'4—dc20   90-14253
ISBN 0-19-434376-6

Acquisitions Editor: Susan Lanzano
Senior Editor: Ellen Lehrburger
Editor: Jane Sturtevant
Associate Editor: Ken Mencz
Design Manager: Lynn Luchetti
Art Buyer/Picture Researcher: Paula Radding
Production Controller: Abram Hall

Cover Illustration by Dennis Ziemienski
Continuing characters illustrated by Bob Marstall. Other interior
illustrations by Peter Bono, Dave Cutler, Gerry Gersten, Jody Jobe, Karin
Kretschmann, Nina Laden, Mike Lester, Mary Martylewski, Patrick Merrell,
Stephanie O'Shaughnessy, Lori Osiecki, Claudia Karabaic Sargent, and
Brian Schatell.

Graphics and realia by Leslie Nolan and Stephan Van Litsenborg.

Printing (last digit): 10 9 8 7 6 5 4 3 2

Printed in United States.

CROSSROADS 1

STUDENT BOOK

Irene Frankel
Cliff Meyers

with

Earl W. Stevick

Oxford University Press

Acknowledgements

Thanks to the reviewers, field-testers, and consultants who helped to shape this book:

Deborah Adams, Houston Community College, Houston, Texas

Dr. Virginia French Allen, Professor Emeritus, Temple University, Philadelphia, Pennsylvania

Fiona Armstrong, New York, New York

Ann Creighton, Los Angeles Unified School District, Los Angeles, California

Burna Dunn, Teikyo Loretto Heights University, Denver, Colorado

Annamaria Gallo, FDR High School, Brooklyn, New York

Rheta R. Goldman, Los Angeles Unified School District, Los Angeles, California

Mary Jeannot, University of Massachusetts, Amherst, Massachusetts

Autumn Keltner, Sacramento, California

Penny Larson, San Francisco Community College District, San Francisco, California

Manuel Menendez, New York City Public Schools, New York, New York

Yvonne Nishio, Evans Community Adult School, Los Angeles, California

Susan Prior, The Riverside Adult Learning Center, New York, New York

Kathleen Santopietro, Colorado Department of Education, Denver, Colorado

Rochelle Yarish, Gene A. Whiddon Adult Center, Fort Lauderdale, Florida.

Thanks to Susan Lanzano, Acquisitions Editor, for so lovingly nurturing this project; Ellen Lehrburger, Senior Editor, for lifting us beyond our limitations; Jane Sturtevant, Editor, for treating this book with so much TLC; Ken Mencz, Associate Editor, for so carefully scrutinizing our text; and everyone else at Oxford, especially Paul Phillips.

Thanks to Shirley Brod and Barbara Sample of the Spring Institute for International Studies for their openness, insights, and ever-flowing ideas.

Thanks to Margot Gramer and Dr. Jenny Rardin for their unique contributions to this book, and to Paul Kirchner and the late Dr. Caleb Gattegno for their guidance and inspiration.

This book is dedicated to our mothers, Valerie Meyers and Evelyn Frankel, who cheered us on from the sidelines, to our fathers, Harlan Meyers and Irving Frankel, who smiled down on us from above, and to our partners, Fumi Matsutani and David Martin, who loved and supported us.

Contents

To the Teacher

Crossroads

- is a four-level adult series in English as a second language
- integrates a competency-based approach with systematic grammar presentation
- covers the four skills of listening, speaking, reading, and writing
- is for adults and young adults in adult education or continuing education programs
- begins lower and progresses more gradually than other beginning series
- provides an exceptionally complete and flexible array of classwork, homework, and teacher support materials through the Student Book, Teacher's Book, Multilevel Activity and Resource Package, and Cassettes.

The **Student Book** has ten units with the following sections:

Getting Started	topic opener, prediction
Conversations	new competencies, grammar, vocabulary
Listening Plus	listening skills, clarification strategies
Paperwork	document literacy
Reading and Writing	literacy skills
Interactions	information gap
Progress Checks	competency test

The **Teacher's Book** provides:
- warm-up activities
- step-by-step procedures for each exercise
- suggestions for varying and extending the exercises
- ways to teach pronunciation
- cross-cultural and linguistic notes
- a selection of reproducible visuals
- reproducible Competency Checklists

The **Multilevel Activity and Resource Package** is reproducible and includes:
- listening, grammar, and writing worksheets in two versions, for lower– and higher– level students
- pictures for language experience stories
- games
- student-to-student dictations and mixer activities
- punctuation and handwriting worksheets
- word cards, picture cards, and game boards
- practical teaching notes

Placement

Place students in CROSSROADS 1 if they function minimally or not at all in English.

Place students in CROSSROADS 2 if they are able to function in a very limited way, depending largely on learned phrases.

Place students in CROSSROADS 3 if they have moved beyond learned phrases and are beginning to function with some independence and creativity, but still have difficulty communicating even with someone who is used to dealing with people of limited English proficiency.

Place students in CROSSROADS 4 if they can communicate, though with some difficulty, on familiar topics with native speakers who are *not* accustomed to dealing with people of limited English proficiency.

CROSSROADS is compatible with the Comprehensive Adult Student Assessment System (CASAS) and the Student Performance Levels (SPL's) recommended by the Mainstream English Language Training (MELT) Project of the U.S. Department of Health and Human Services. SPL's are correlated with scores on the Basic English Skills Test (BEST).

	MELT SPL's	BEST Scores	CASAS Achievement Scores
CROSSROADS 1	I and II	9–28	165–190
CROSSROADS 2	III	29–41	191–196
CROSSROADS 3	IV and V	42–57	197–210
CROSSROADS 4	VI and VII	58–65+	211–224

Placement can also be made according to students' control of grammar. CROSSROADS 1 covers the present tense of *be,* the present continuous tense, and the simple present tense. CROSSROADS 2 covers the past tense of *be* and regular verbs, and the future with *be going to.* CROSSROADS 3 covers the past tense with irregular verbs, the future tense with *will,* and the past progressive tense. CROSSROADS 4 covers the present perfect and present perfect continuous tenses.

One of these symbols in the margin next to an exercise tells you that a specific competency is first practiced there. In the *Progress Checks* pages, the same letter identifies the exercise that tests that competency.

Teaching Procedures

An underlying principle of CROSSROADS is "elicit before you teach." Before students at this level tackle print, we suggest that they guess what the text might say, share any language they already know about the topic, listen to the text on cassette or read by their teacher, and learn or review key vocabulary. Similarly, before attempting independent pair practice, students might repeat the exercise aloud together, learn needed vocabulary, and participate in supervised pair practice.

Most instruction lines recur throughout the book and stand for, rather than spell out, complete teaching procedures. **Step-by-Step Teaching Procedures** for these recurring exercises appear on pages x–xiii, following this introduction. They state the purpose of the exercise and include preparation and follow-up to help students progress at their own pace, and to make written materials accessible to students with limited literacy skills.

Most exercises correspond to one of the Step-by-Step Teaching Procedures. Those that do not are covered in the Teacher's Book, which provides an individually-tailored procedure for every Student Book exercise.

Many of the exercises in CROSSROADS ask students to provide information about themselves. Most students enjoy this and feel that it helps them learn. However, there may be times when students are unwilling or unable to supply personal information. Therefore, several of the teaching procedures suggest that students may provide fictitious rather than true information.

Progress Checks

The last two pages of each unit allow both you and the students to find out how well they have mastered the material presented in the unit. Each exercise requires students to demonstrate specific competencies.

Spoken competencies (sometimes in combination with certain competencies in reading and writing) are tested in two-part, pair-work exercises. In the first part of the exercise ("What are the people saying?"), pictures help students generate conversations with language they learned in the unit. For your convenience, **Basic Conversations** which students may generate are supplied on pages 129–130. In the second part of the exercise ("Do it yourself."), students use the same conversations with their own information in order to demonstrate competency.

Competencies in document literacy are demonstrated as students read and complete forms similar to those they worked within the unit. Competencies in identifying things and following instructions are demonstrated in matching or circling exercises.

The *Progress Checks* can be used in a number of ways, depending on your priorities and needs. Since the exercises can be done as individual or pair work, students can use these pages for self-directed review, checking off each competency when they feel ready. If, on the other hand, you require a more controlled assessment, you can check students individually. The Teacher's Book supplies reproducible checklists of the competencies for each unit.

If your program is grammar-based, you can emphasize the first part ("What are the people saying?") of the spoken exercises. In generating appropriate, correct conversations to fit the pictures, students utilize all they have learned about the structure of English.

Culminating Activities

Each unit of the Student Book ends with a culminating activity that helps students integrate their newly-acquired competencies into their lives outside the classroom. These activities encourage students to draw upon all of their communicative resources and to exercise their creativity.

The Grammar Summaries

The Grammar Summaries on pages 121–123 present complete paradigms of the grammatical structures featured in the Student Book, including those highlighted in "Focus on grammar" exercises.

Step-by-Step Teaching Procedures
(in alphabetical order)

Check what you hear.

Gives practice with new vocabulary; introduces a clarification strategy.
1. Copy the speech bubbles onto the board.
2. Read the conversation aloud at normal speed. Point to each bubble as you say the words in it.
3. Say the conversation line by line and have students repeat after you.
4. Show students where to find the cues.
5. Have pairs of students say the conversation for the class, using all the cues.
6. Have students practice the conversation in pairs. Each student should practice both parts and use all the cues.

Fill in the form.

Gives practice in reading and filling in forms.
Note: Students may want or need to give fictitious information about themselves. Show that this is acceptable by repeating Step 2, giving obviously fictitious information about yourself.
1. Reproduce the blank form on the board or use an overhead projector.
2. Fill in the form one blank at a time with information about yourself. After filling in each blank, make a statement about yourself with the information you have just written.
3. Erase your information. Interview a volunteer and fill in the form again. Leave the filled-in form on the board for students to use as a model.
4. Have students fill in the forms in their books with their own information.
5. Have students compare their answers in pairs.

Focus on grammar.

Helps students to infer grammatical principles without using grammar terms.
1. From the box, choose a pair of items that contrast *(Where is the book? / Where are the books?* or *Where is the book? / It's on the shelf.).* Write the pair side by side on the board or use an overhead projector.
2. Read the two items aloud and have students repeat.
3. Provide another example like the left-hand item in the box *(Where is the chair?),* write it underneath, and have students repeat.

4. Elicit the corresponding item for the right-hand column *(Where are the chairs?),* write it, and have students repeat.
5. Point to the next space in the right-hand column and elicit an example to fill it.
6. Elicit the corresponding item for the left-hand column.
7. Have students copy the items on a separate piece of paper.
8. Use the same procedure for the other contrasting pairs in the box.

Get information. / Give information.
Give directions. / Follow directions.
Give instructions. / Follow instructions.

On the *Interactions* pages, provides an information gap for communicative practice of grammar and vocabulary.
1. Write the conversation on the board or use an overhead projector. Don't fill in the handwritten parts yet.
2. Review the vocabulary students will be using in the exercise.
3. Hold up your book and show students that there are two pages.
4. Divide the class into a Student A group and a Student B group. Have them open their books to the appropriate page.
5. Show students where in the book Students A and B get their information.
6. Fill in the blanks in the conversation on the board and read the conversation aloud.
7. Call on volunteers from the two groups to say the conversation.
8. Erase the information in the blanks. Call on other volunteers to say the conversation using the next cue. Fill in the blanks.
9. Have A's work with B's in pairs to do the exercises and fill in the information. Each student should change roles and do both pages.
10. Go over the answers with the whole class.

Guess.

Provides a context for the unit.
1. Give students a little time to look at the picture.
2. Have students identify the characters, or identify them yourself.

3. Ask where the characters are.
4. Ask students to guess what the characters are saying. All responses are valid here.
5. Respond to each guess by restating it in acceptable English.

Interview three classmates.

Gives practice in speaking and writing.
Note: Students may want or need to give fictitious information about themselves. Show that this is acceptable by repeating Step 4, giving obviously fictitious information about yourself.
1. Copy the questions on the board or overhead projector. Don't fill in the answers yet.
2. Invite a student to speak for the character in the conversation at the top of the page whose information is given as the example in the book. Interview the volunteer and fill in the example with students' help.
3. Say the interview questions one at a time and have students repeat them.
4. Erase the answers. Invite a student to interview you and write your answers on the board.
5. Correct the answers with the whole class.
6. Have students ask and answer the questions with three classmates.

Practice. *(the first conversation in the unit)*

Introduces specific competencies, vocabulary, and/or grammar.
1. Play the tape or read the conversation aloud while students follow along silently in their books.
2. Use the pictures on the previous page or otherwise elicit or demonstrate the meaning of key words and phrases.
3. Have students repeat the conversation chorally— line by line.
4. Have them practice in pairs.

Practice. *(after the first one in the unit)*

Introduces specific competencies, vocabulary, and/or grammar.
1. Give students a little time to look at the visual.
2. Encourage them to guess the conversation.
3. Have students close their books. Play the tape or read the conversation aloud. Use visuals to indicate which character is speaking each line.
4. Have students say anything they can recall of the conversation. Acknowledge all contributions by restating them in acceptable English.
5. Play the tape or read the conversation aloud while students follow along silently in their books.
6. Using visuals or other means, elicit or demonstrate the meaning of key words and phrases.
7. Have students repeat the conversation chorally—line by line.
8. Have them practice in pairs.

Read _____'s story. / Read about _____.

Provides practice in reading prose.
1. Give students a few minutes to look at the story and read what they can.
2. Play the tape or read the story aloud while students follow along silently in their books
3. Play the tape or read the story one line at a time and have students repeat it chorally.
4. Ask volunteers to read single lines of the story aloud.

Read your story to your group.

Lets students share their writing.
1. Have a volunteer read his/her story aloud to the class.
2. Have the class restate the story to confirm understanding. Encourage the volunteer to clarify meaning, if necessary.
3. Lead the class in applause for the reader.
4. Have students work in groups to read their stories in turn and to receive responses and applause from their peers.
5. Have students copy their stories on a separate piece of paper.
6. "Publish" the stories by posting them in the classroom.

Say...Repeat...Point.

Introduces vocabulary and sometimes a competency; gives practice in listening for specific information.

Say.
1. Have students say any words they already know.
2. Use the board or an overhead projector. As each word is volunteered, write it in a place corresponding to its location in the book.
3. Pronounce each word after you write it. Have students point to the word in their books and repeat it.
4. In the same way, add any words that students have not volunteered. Leave the words on the board for **Repeat** and **Point**.

Repeat.
1. Play the tape or read the first item aloud. Point to each item on the board as students hear it.
2. Play the tape or read the tapescript again item by item. Point to each item on the board or overhead projector and have students repeat chorally.

Point.

Note: Beginning in Unit 3, students hear short conversations beyond the level they are expected to produce or even completely understand. They should listen for specific information only.

1. Play the tape or read the first word or conversation in the tapescript aloud. Point to the target word on the board as students hear it in the conversation.
2. Play the tape or read the rest of the tapescript for that exercise aloud, conversation by conversation. Have students point to the target item in their books and a volunteer point to the item on the board so that students can check their answers.
3. Have students copy the items onto a separate piece of paper, practice writing each item several times, and then dictate the items to each other in pairs.

Talk about _____.

Provides practice with competencies, grammar, and vocabulary.

1. Write the conversation on the board or use an overhead projector. Don't fill in the handwritten parts yet.
2. Show students where to get the information for the first blank and fill it in. Do the same with the other blanks.
3. Read the filled-in conversation aloud line by line and have students repeat.
4. Read the cues aloud one by one and have students repeat.
5. Have pairs of students say the conversation for the class with the cues until all the cues have been used.
6. Have students practice the conversation in pairs. Each student should change partners at least once, say both parts, and use all the cues.

Talk about your_____ / yourself.

Provides practice with competencies, grammar, and vocabulary.

Note: Students may want or need to give fictitious information about themselves. Show that this is acceptable by repeating Steps 3 and 4, giving obviously fictitious information about yourself.

1. Write the conversation on the board or use an overhead projector. Don't fill in the handwritten parts.
2. If there are cues, read them aloud one by one and have students repeat.
3. Fill in the blanks one by one for yourself and a volunteer. If there are cues, show students where to find them.

4. Read the filled-in conversation aloud line by line and have students repeat. Then have the volunteer say the conversation with you.
5. Replace the filled-in parts of the conversation with new information about two more volunteers. Have the volunteers say the conversation for the class.
6. Have other pairs of students say the conversation for the class. If there are cues, use them all.
7. Have students practice in pairs. Each student should change partners at least once, say both parts, and use all the cues.

What are the people saying?/Do it yourself.

Provides for spoken demonstration of competency. See page ix, and in the Teacher's Book, page viii.

What are the people saying?

1. Have students work in pairs to identify the situation, the relationship of the people, and what the people are saying. Circulate to give help and feedback.
2. Have students work in two-pair groups to compare their answers and conversations.
3. Have volunteers act out the conversation for the class. Have the other students approve what they say or suggest changes.

Do it yourself.

1. Have students say both parts of the conversation with partners, using their own information and/or whatever cues are supplied.
2. When a student has successfully demonstrated a competency, it can be checked off and dated or initialed.

What can you hear?

Prepares students to read the first conversation in the unit.

1. Have students look at the picture while you play the tape or read the conversation aloud.
2. Have students volunteer any words or sentences they can recall from the conversation.
3. Acknowledge all contributions by restating them in acceptable English.
4. Let them hear the conversation again to elicit more pieces of it.

What can you say?

Adds to vocabulary introduced in **Practice**.
1. Ask students to look at the picture(s) and tell you any words they can read or guess.
2. Use the board or overhead projector. As each word is volunteered, write it in a place corresponding to its location in the book.
3. Pronounce each word after you write it. Have students point to the word in their books and repeat it.
4. In the same way, add any words students have not volunteered.
5. Ask a volunteer to stand and hold up the book for the class to see, or use an overhead projector. For each word, call on one volunteer to say the word and another volunteer to point to the picture for the class.
6. Have students work in pairs, one saying a word and the other pointing.
7. Have students copy the words onto a separate piece of paper, practice writing each word several times, and then dictate the words to each other in pairs.

What can you say about _____?

Prepares students for the reading which follows.
1. Have students look at the visual and say any words or sentences they can about it.
2. As each key word, phrase, or sentence is suggested, write it on the board or use an overhead projector. Say the item and have students repeat it.
3. Add any key words, phrases, or sentences from the reading that follows that students have not volunteered.
4. Point to items on the board at random and have students read them aloud.

Write about yourself.

Gives practice in multi-sentence writing.
Note: Students may want or need to give fictitious information about themselves. Show that this is acceptable by repeating Steps 1 and 3, giving obviously fictitious information about yourself.
1. Tell your own story to the class, using the story on the preceding page as a model.
2. Help students restate what you have said to confirm their understanding.

3. Write your story on the board or overhead projector. Leave it for students to use as a model for their own writing in Step 5.
4. Have students work in pairs and tell their stories to each other. After the first student talks, the other student restates the story to confirm understanding. Then they switch roles.
5. Have students write their stories. Encourage them to help each other. Circulate to give help as needed or to listen to students' stories.

Write / Fill in the _____ you hear.

Gives practice in listening for specific information and writing.
Note: As in **Point,** students hear short conversations beyond the level they are expected to produce or even completely understand. They should listen for specific information only.
1. Copy the answer blanks on the board or use an overhead projector.
2. Play the tape or read the first conversation in the tapescript aloud. Write the first answer on the board when students hear it.
3. Continue with one conversation at a time and have students write their answers in their books.
4. Have students compare their answers in pairs.
5. Play the tape or read the tapescript aloud again, one conversation at a time. Have a volunteer write his/her answers on the board and have the other students correct any errors.
6. Have students check their answers against the correct answers on the board.
7. Let students hear the conversations once more to verify their answers.

Han Fu Chang

Babacar Diop

Victor Gomez

Sara Gilbert

Neary Som

Anna Skalska

Yuki Sato

Pablo Burgos

Carmen Soto

Marie Duval

Rosa Sanchez

Trong Lam

**Westside Community Adult School
Level 1
Sara Gilbert's Class**

Introductions

Getting Started

1. Guess. What are Rosa and Han Fu saying?

2. What can you hear?

Conversations _____

1. Practice.

Rosa:	Hi. I'm Rosa Sanchez.
Han Fu:	Hi. I'm Han Fu Chang.
Rosa:	Nice to meet you.
Han Fu:	Nice to meet you, too.

a **2. Talk about yourself. Meet five people.**

A: Hi. I'm _____.

B: Hi. I'm _____.

A: Nice to meet you.

B: Nice to meet you, too.

3. Practice.

4. Talk about yourself. Meet five people.

A: Hi. My name is _____.

What's your name?

B: My name is _____.

Conversations

5. Practice.

Anna Skalska

Her first name is Anna.
Her last name is Skalska.

Victor Gomez

His first name is Victor.
His last name is Gomez.

b

6. Write your first name and last name.

First Name	*Last Name*
Anna	Skalska
Victor	Gomez
Han Fu	Chang

c
d

7. Talk about yourself.

A: What's your first name?

B: My first name is ——————————.

A: What's your last name?

B: My last name is ——————————.

8. Play the Name Game.

Conversations _____

9. Practice.

Rosa	Anna	Sara	Victor	Han Fu
Peru	Poland	the United States	Colombia	China

10. Talk about the people in 9. Use the conversations in 9.

11. Focus on grammar.

I am = I'm
you are = you're
he is = he's
she is = she's

	from Peru.
I'm	
You're	
He's	
She's	

	name is _____.
My	
Your	
His	
Her	

12. Practice.

Anna: Victor, this is Rosa Sanchez.
         Rosa, this is Victor Gomez.
Victor: Hi, Rosa. Nice to meet you.
Rosa: Hi, Victor. Nice to meet you, too.
         Where are you from?
Victor: I'm from Colombia. And you?
Rosa: I'm from Peru.

e
f
g

13. Talk about yourself. Use the conversation in 12.

Listening Plus _____

1. Say . . . Repeat.

A B C D E F G H I J K L M N O P Q R S T U V W X Y Z

a b c d e f g h i j k l m n o p q r s t u v w x y z

2. Repeat . . . Point.

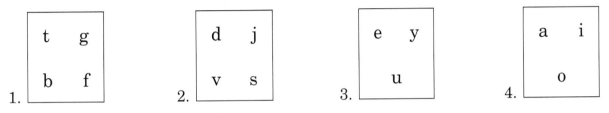

1. t g
    b f

2. d j
    v s

3. e y
       u

4. a i
       o

3. Student A, say a letter. Student B, point. Use the letters in 2.

4. Write the letters you hear.

1. C armen   2. ____ ____ ang   3. Nea ____ ____

4. Yu ____ ____   5. Go ____ ____ ____   6. Ma ____ ____ ____

7. Pa ____ ____ ____   8. Baba ____ ____ ____

5. Check what you hear. Use the names in 4.

Carmen.

How do you spell that?

C-A-R-M-E-N.

Unit 1

5

Paperwork

1. Practice.

Sara: What's your first name?
Pablo: Pablo.
Sara: What's your last name?
Pablo: Burgos.
Sara: Excuse me?
Pablo: Burgos.
Sara: How do you spell that?
Pablo: B-U-R-G-O-S.
Sara: Thank you. Where are you from, Pablo?
Pablo: I'm from Mexico.

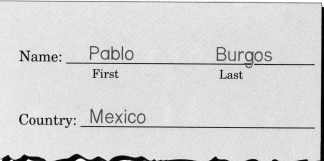

Name: ___Pablo_____Burgos_____
         First   Last

Country: ___Mexico_____

2. Fill in the form.

Name: _____
         First   Last

Country: _____

3. Interview three classmates.

	Pablo	Student A	Student B	Student C
What's your first name?	Pablo			
What's your last name?	Burgos			
Where are you from?	Mexico			

Classroom Skills _____

1. What can you say?

book   pen   pencil   door

board   clock   notebook   window

2. a. Write the words in 1 on separate pieces of paper.
      b. Listen to your teacher. Hold up the word you hear.

3. Label the things in your classroom. Use the pieces of paper from 2.

4. Practice.

> What's the word for this in English?
>
> Window.
>
> Excuse me?
>
> Window.

5. Walk around your classroom. Talk about the things you see.
     Use the conversation in 4.

Classroom Skills

6. Listen to your teacher. Follow the instructions.

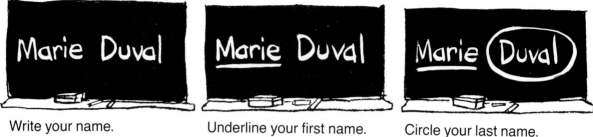

Write your name.

Underline your first name.

Circle your last name.

i **7. Student A, spell your first and last names. Student B, write.**

8. Listen to your teacher. Follow the instructions.

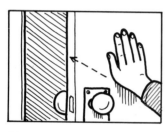

Close the door.

Open your notebook.

Look at the board.

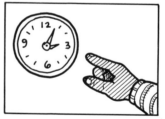

Point to the clock.

j **9. Student A, give instructions. Student B, follow the instructions.**

Close	the door.
Open	your book.
Point to	your notebook.
Look at	the window.

8

Interactions

Student A

1. **Give instructions. Tell B to write the words.**

   A: In Box C, write __teacher__ .

   B: How do you spell that?

   A: T-E-A-C-H-E-R .

   B: T-E-A-C-H-E-R. Teacher .

C	D	E
teacher	_____	pencil
F	**G**	**H**
_____	window	_____
I	**J**	**K**
book	_____	door
L	**M**	**N**
_____	first	_____

2. **Follow instructions. Fill in the blanks.**

Interactions _____
Student B

1. **Follow instructions. Fill in the blanks.**

   A: In Box C, write ___teacher___ .

   B: How do you spell that?

   A: ___T-E-A-C-H-E-R___ .

   B: ___T-E-A-C-H-E-R.   Teacher___ .

C	D	E
___teacher___	pen	_____
F	**G**	**H**
name	_____	last
I	**J**	**K**
_____	clock	_____
L	**M**	**N**
notebook	_____	board

2. **Give instructions. Tell A to write the words.**

Progress Checks

1. **b** ☐ Write your first and last name.

   Fill in the form.

   Name: _____

          Last   *First*

2. **c** ☐ Ask someone's first and last name.
   d ☐ Give your first and last name.
   i ☐ Spell your first and last name.

   What are the people saying?

   Do it yourself.

3. **h** ☐ Identify things in a classroom.
   j ☐ Follow classroom instructions.

   What are the people saying?

   Do it yourself.

Progress Checks ✔

4. **a** ☐ Introduce yourself.
   f ☐ Introduce others.
   e ☐ Ask where someone is from.
   g ☐ Say where you are from.

What are the people saying?

Do it yourself.

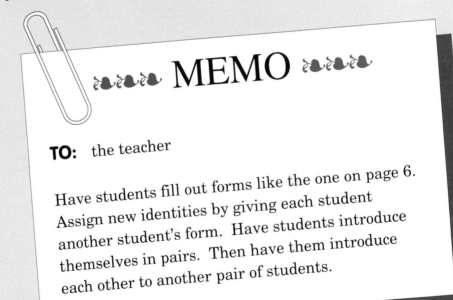

❧❧❧❧❧ MEMO *❧❧❧❧❧*

TO: the teacher

Have students fill out forms like the one on page 6. Assign new identities by giving each student another student's form. Have students introduce themselves in pairs. Then have them introduce each other to another pair of students.

Getting Started _____

1. Guess. What are Carmen and Neary saying?

2. What can you hear?

Conversations _____

[cassette icon] **1. Practice.**

Carmen: Hi, Neary. How are you?
Neary: Fine, thanks. And you?
Carmen: I'm fine.
Neary: Carmen, my brother and sister are here now.
Carmen: Oh, really?
Neary: Yes. This is a picture of my family.

a **2. Talk about yourself.**

A: Hi, _____. How are you?

B: Fine, thanks. And you?

A: I'm fine.

3. What can you say?

sister   mother   father   brother

[cassette icon] **4. Practice.**

Carmen: Who's that?
Neary: That's my brother.
Carmen: What's his name?
Neary: His name is Dara.

5. Focus on grammar.

who is	= who's
that is	= that's
what is	= what's

6. Draw a picture of your father, mother, brothers, and sisters. Use a separate piece of paper.

b c d e **7. Talk about your picture. Use the conversation in 4.**

Conversations

8. Practice.

David

A: Who's that?
B: He's my friend.
A: What's his name?
B: His name is David.
A: Where is he from?
B: He's from Los Angeles.

Elena and Rita

A: Who are those people?
B: They're my friends.
A: What are their names?
B: Their names are Elena and Rita.
A: Where are they from?
B: They're from Mexico.

9. Focus on grammar.

> they are = they're

10. Draw your friends. Write their names.

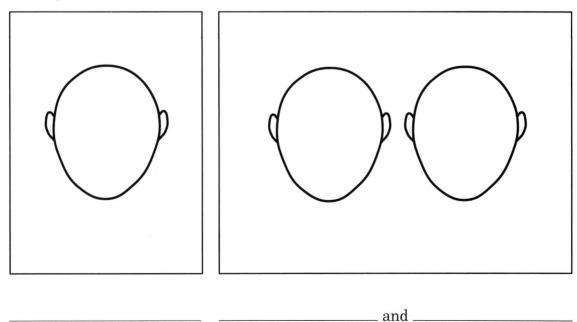

_____   _____ and _____

11. Talk about your friends. Use the conversations in 8.

Conversations _____

12. Practice.

Carmen: Here, Neary. This is my family.
Neary: Oh. Who's that?
Carmen: That's my son, Albert.
Neary: Oh, really? Is he married?
Carmen: Yes, he is. And this is Marta.
Neary: Is she Albert's wife?
Carmen: No, she's not. She's my daughter.
Neary: Where is your husband?
Carmen: My husband is dead.
Neary: I'm sorry, Carmen.

13. Focus on grammar.

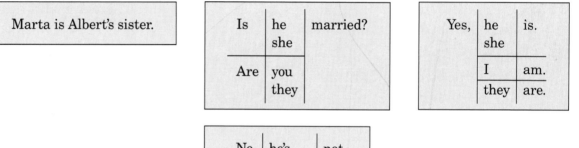

Marta is Albert's sister.

Is	he	married?
	she	
Are	you	
	they	

Yes,	he	is.
	she	
	I	am.
	they	are.

No,	he's	not.
	she's	
	I'm	
	they're	

14. What can you say?

husband   wife   son   son   daughter

15. Talk about Pablo's family.

A: Is _____Nora_____ his _____wife_____?

B: _____No, she's not. She's his daughter_____.

16

Listening Plus

1. **Say . . . Repeat . . . Point.**

   0 1 2 3 4 5 6 7 8 9 10

2. **Point.**

2	4	
6	8	10

   0

1	3	
5	7	9

3. **Student A, say a number. Student B, point. Use the numbers in 1.**

4. **Fill in the area codes you hear.**

   a. 2 _1_ 3   b. 2 __ 2   c. __ 1 __

   d. __ 0 __   e. __ 0 __   f. __ 1 __

5. **Fill in the phone numbers you hear.**

   a. _3_ _2_ _6_ - 3589   b. __ __ __ - 7871   c. __ __ __ - 9966

   d. (713) __ __ __ - 6029   e. (212) 362 - __ __ __ __

   f. (312) 692 - __ __ __ __

6. **Check what you hear. Use the phone numbers in 5.**

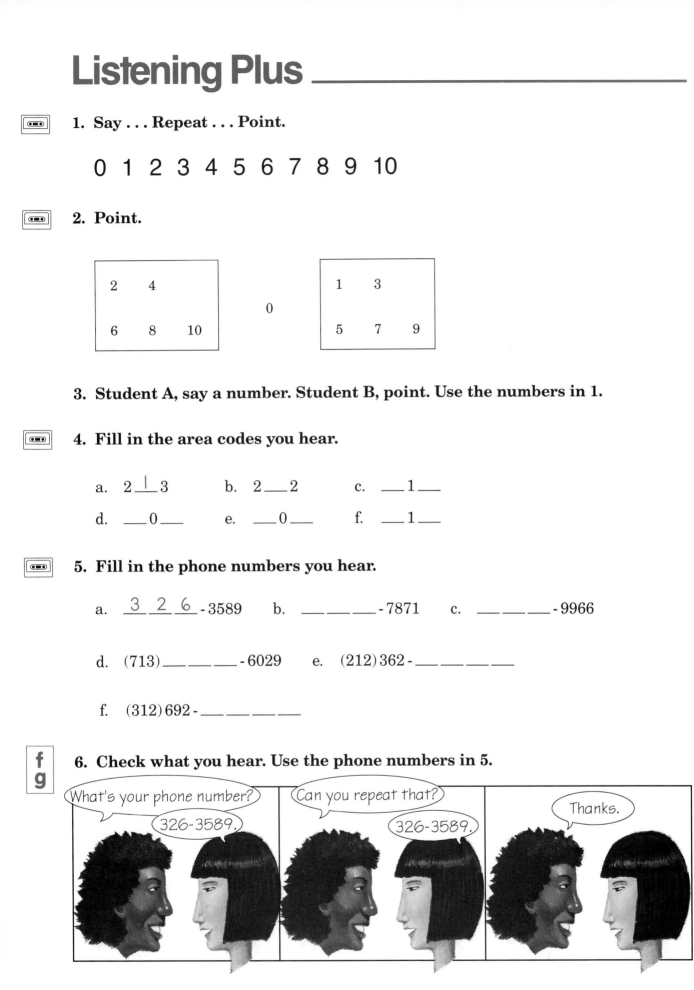

What's your phone number?

326-3589.

Can you repeat that?

326-3589.

Thanks.

Paperwork

1. Practice.

Sara: Hello. I'm Sara Gilbert. What's your name?

Trong: Trong Lam.

Sara: Where are you from, Trong?

Trong: I'm from Vietnam.

Sara: What's your phone number?

Trong: 655-9238.

Sara: Can you repeat that?

Trong: 655-9238.

Sara: And what's your area code?

Trong: 209.

Name: __Lam__ __Trong__
          Last   First

Country: __Vietnam__

Phone number: (_209_) _655-9238_
            Area code

h   **2. Fill in the form.**

Name: _____
       Last   First

Country: _____

Phone number: (_____)_____
          Area code

i
j   **3. Interview three classmates.**

	Trong	Student A	Student B	Student C
What's your name?	Trong Lam			
Where are you from?	Vietnam			
What's your phone number?	655-9238			
What's your area code?	209			

Reading and Writing _____

1. **What can you say about Victor's family? Who are the people?
    Fill in the blanks.**

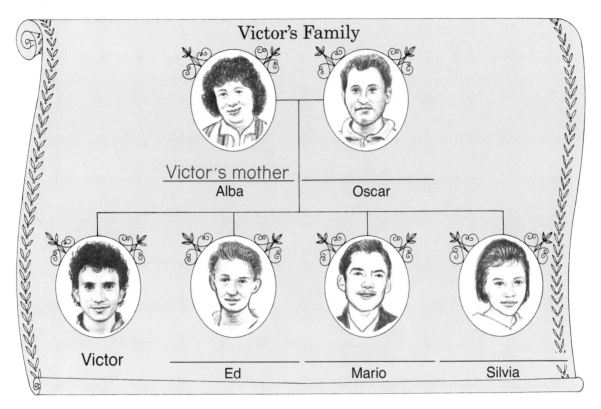

Victor's Family

Victor's mother
Alba

Oscar

Victor

Ed

Mario

Silvia

2. **Read Victor's story.**

    My name is Victor Gomez.
    This is my family.
    This is my mother, Alba.
    This is my father, Oscar.
    This is my brother, Ed.
    This is my brother, Mario.
    And this is my sister, Silvia.

3. **Circle the correct sentence.
    Write the sentences on a separate piece of paper.**

    a. Who is Ed?   Ed is Victor's brother.   Ed is Victor's father.

    b. Who is Alba?   Alba is Victor's sister.   Alba is Victor's mother.

    c. Who is Silvia?   Silvia is Victor's brother.   Silvia is Victor's sister.

    d. Who is Oscar?   Oscar is Victor's father.   Oscar is Victor's mother.

Reading and Writing _____

4. What can you say about Marie's family? Who are the people?
Fill in the blanks.

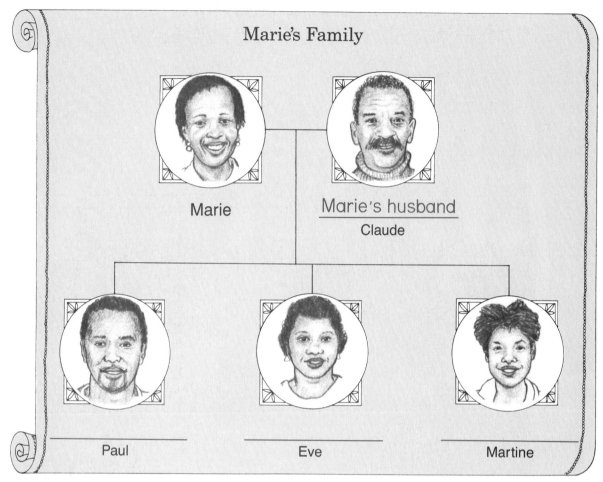

Marie's Family

Marie

Marie's husband
Claude

Paul   Eve   Martine

5. Read Marie's story.

I am Marie Duval.
This is my family.
This is my husband, Claude.
This is my son, Paul.
This is my daughter, Eve.
And this is my daughter, Martine.

6. Fill in the blanks. Write the sentences on a separate piece of paper.

a. Who is Claude? __He__ is Marie's __husband__ .

b. Who are Martine and Eve? _____ are Marie's _____ .

c. Who is Paul? _____ is Marie's _____ .

Interactions

Student A

1. **Get and give information about Susan's family.**
   Ask about: Mary, John, Bobby, Ray, and Laura.

   A: Is ___Mary Susan's daughter___?

   B: ___No, she's not___.

   A: Is ___Mary___ her ___mother___?

   B: ___Yes, she is___.

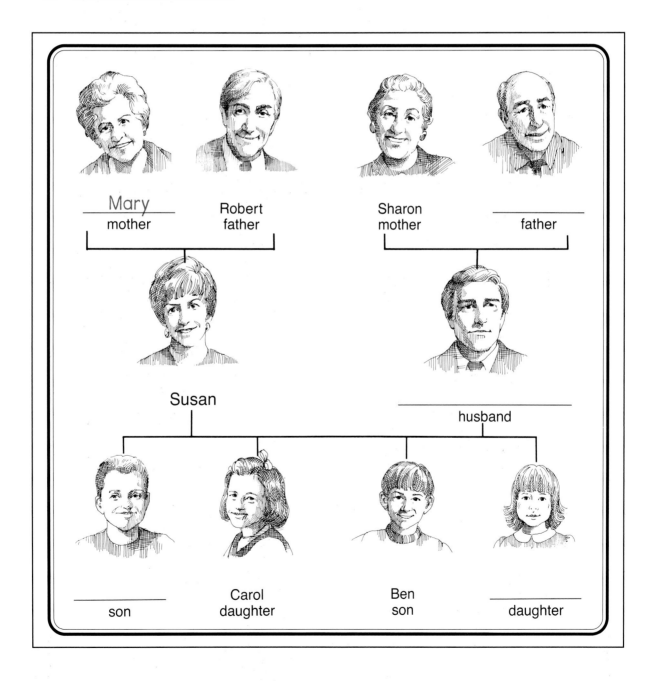

Interactions

Student B

1. **Get and give information about Susan's family.**
   Ask about: Carol, Sharon, Robert, and Ben.

   A: Is <u>Mary Susan's daughter</u>?

   B: <u>No, she's not</u>.

   A: Is <u>Mary</u> her <u>mother</u>?

   B: <u>Yes, she is</u>.

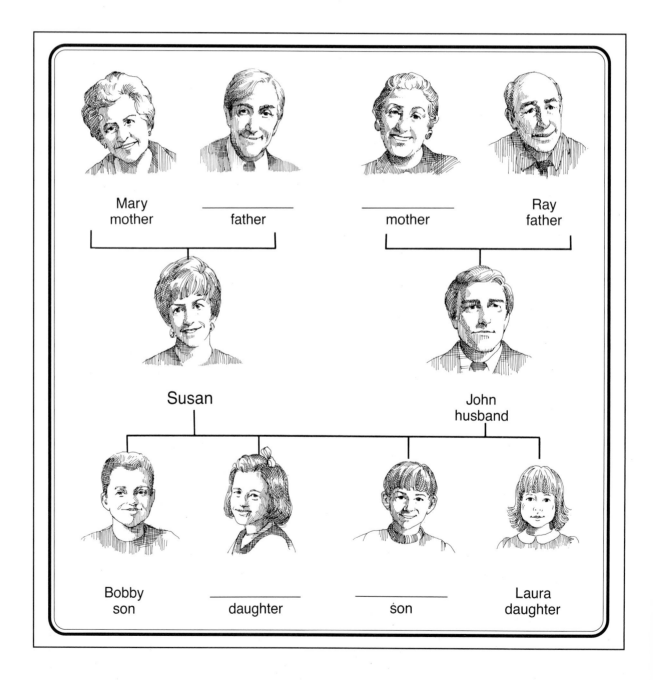

Mary
mother

_____
father

_____
mother

Ray
father

Susan

John
husband

Bobby
son

_____
daughter

_____
son

Laura
daughter

Progress Checks

1. **h** ☐ Write your phone number and area code.

   Fill in the form.

   Name: _____
          Last   *First*

   Telephone Number: (_____) _____
                     area code

2. **i** ☐ Ask for someone's area code and phone number.
   j ☐ Give your area code and phone number.
   f ☐ Ask someone to repeat.
   g ☐ Repeat when someone asks you to.

   What are the people saying?

   Do it yourself.

3. **a** ☐ Greet someone.

   What are the people saying?

   Do it yourself.

Progress Checks

4. **b** ☐ Ask about the people in a family.
   c ☐ Give relationships in your family.
   d ☐ Ask for names of family members.
   e ☐ Name the people in your family.

What are the people saying?

Do it yourself. Show pictures of your family.

๕๕๕๕ MEMO ๕๕๕๕

TO: the teacher

Divide the class into "families." Have each family decide what their relationships are. Have the other students ask the family members questions ("Are you Kim's mother?") to try to figure out all the relationships in the family.

3 School

Getting Started _____

1. Guess. What are Sara, Trong, and Rosa saying?

2. What can you hear?

Conversations _____

1. Practice.

Sara: Trong, would you please close the door?
Trong: OK.
Sara: And Rosa, would you get the books, please?
Rosa: OK. Where are they?
Sara: They're on the shelf. Thanks.

2. What can you say?

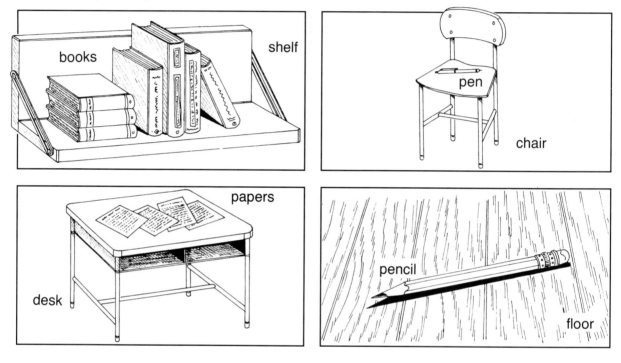

books   shelf

pen

chair

papers

desk

pencil

floor

3. Focus on grammar.

Where	is	the book?
	are	the books?

It's They're	on the shelf.

it is = it's

4. Talk about the pictures in 2.

A: Where is the __pen__ ?

B: It's on the __chair__ .

A: Where are the __books__ ?

B: They're on the __shelf__ .

5. Talk about your classroom. Use the conversations in 4.

a
b

26   Unit 3

Conversations _____

6. Practice.

Yuki: Excuse me. Where is the office?
Trong: The office? It's next to Room 103.
Yuki: Where?
Rosa: Over there.
Yuki: Oh. Thanks.

7. What can you say?

the exit	Room 101	Room 103	the office
Room 102	the ladies' room	Room 104	the men's room

**8. Talk about places in school. Use the floor plan in 7.
Use the conversation in 6.**

**9. Draw a floor plan of one floor of your school.
Talk about places in your school.**

A: Where is __the exit__?

B: __The exit__? It's next to __Room 101__.

Conversations

10. Practice.

Rosa: Hi. Are you a new student?
Yuki: Yes, I am. My name is Yuki.
Rosa: I'm Rosa.
Trong: I'm Trong. Are you in Level 2?
Yuki: No, I'm not.

11. Talk about yourself.

A: Are you __a new student__?

B: __No, I'm not__.

a. a new student b. from Mexico c. a teacher d. from the United States

12. Practice.

Yuki: I'm in Level 1.
Rosa: Really? We're in Level 1.
Yuki: Great! Who's our teacher?
Trong: Her name is Sara. Sara Gilbert.
Rosa: We're on our break now.
Trong: Oh, no! Look at the clock. We're late!

13. Focus on grammar.

we are = we're

Are you in Level 2?

Yes, we are.
No, we're not.

14. Talk about yourself.

a. What level are you in?
b. Are you new students?
c. Who's your teacher?
d. What's your room number?

Listening Plus _____

1. Say . . . Repeat . . . Point.

11   12   13   14   15   16   17   18   19

10   20   30   40   50   60   70   80   90

2. Check what you hear. Use the numbers in 1.

It's 60.

60?

Yes, 60. That's 6-0.

3. Say . . . Repeat . . . Point.

21   22   23   24   25   26   27   28   29

4. Write the number you hear.

		1	2	3	4	5	6	7	8	9
10	ten									
20	twenty		22							
30	thirty									
40	forty									
50	fifty									
60	sixty									
70	seventy									
80	eighty									
90	ninety									

**5. Student A, say a number. Student B, write the number.
Use the chart in 4.**

Paperwork _____

1. Practice.

Sara: Where are you from, Babacar?
Babacar: I'm from Senegal.
Sara: And is your first language French?
Babacar: No, it's not. My first language is Wolof.
Sara: Wolof? W-O-L-O-F?
Babacar: Yes.
Sara: Are you married?
Babacar: Yes, I am.
Sara: How old are you?
Babacar: I'm 35.

Name: __Diop_____Babacar_____
              Last   First

Country: ___Senegal_____

Language: ___Wolof_____

Marital Status: (circle one) (married) single

Age: __35_____

g
h

2. Fill in the form.

Name: _____
             Last   First

Country: _____

Language: _____

Marital Status: (circle one) married   single

Age: _____

i
j

3. Interview three classmates. Guess their languages.

	Babacar	Student A	Student B	Student C
Where are you from?	Senegal			
Is your first language __French__?	Wolof			
Are you married?	married			
How old are you?	35			

Reading and Writing _____

1. Look at Babacar's form. What can you say about Babacar?

2. Read Babacar's story.

My name is Babacar Diop.
I'm from Senegal.
My first language is Wolof.
I'm 35.
I'm married.
I'm a new student.

3. Answer the questions about Babacar. Circle *Yes* or *No*. Write a sentence.

a. Is his last name Babacar?   Yes   (No)   His last name is Diop.

b. Is he from Senegal?   (Yes)   No   He's from Senegal.

c. Is his first language French?   Yes   No   _____

d. Is he 37?   Yes   No   _____

e. Is he married?   Yes   No   _____

f. Is he a new student?   Yes   No   _____

4. Write about yourself. Fill in the blanks.
Use Babacar's story as an example.

My name is _____

I'm from _____

My first language is _____

I'm _____

I'm _____

I'm _____ student.

5. Read your story to your group.

Reading and Writing

6. What can you say about Rosa and Trong's school?

___Westside Community Adult School___
School

(_209_) ___684-1555___   ___|___
School Telephone Number   Level

Teacher: _Sara Gilbert_   Room: ___101___

7. Read about Rosa and Trong's school.

Our school is the Westside Community Adult School.
The phone number is (209) 684-1555.
We're in Level 1.
Our teacher is Sara Gilbert.
Our class is in Room 101.

8. Fill in the form.

_____
School

(_____) _____   _____
School Telephone Number   Level

Teacher: _____   Room: _____

9. Write about your school. Fill in the blanks.

Our school is the _____

The phone number is (_____) _____-_____

We're in _____

Our teacher is _____

Our class is in _____

**10. Copy the information in 9. Use a separate piece of paper.
Keep it at home, next to the phone.**

Interactions _____

Student A

1. **Get information. Write the words. Ask about: the books, the picture, the clock, the chair, the notebook, and the pens.**

   A: Where _are the books_____?

   B: _They're on the shelf_____.

   A: Where _is the picture_____?

   B: _It's next to the door_____.

2. **Give information.**

Interactions

Student B

1. **Give information.**

    A: Where <u>are the books</u>?

    B: <u>They're on the shelf</u>.

    A: Where <u>is the picture</u>?

    B: <u>It's next to the door</u>.

2. **Get information. Write the words.**
   Ask about: the board, the desk, the picture, the papers, and the pencils.

Progress Checks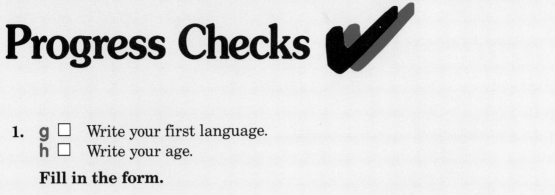

1. **g** ☐ Write your first language.
   h ☐ Write your age.

Fill in the form.

Name _____

First Language _____ Age _____

2. **e** ☐ Give your teacher's name, your class level, and your room number.
   i ☐ Give your first language.
   j ☐ Give your age.
   f ☐ Repeat to check your understanding.

What are the people saying?

Do it yourself.

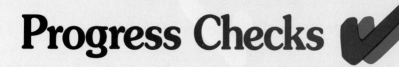

Progress Checks

3. **a** ☐ Ask where things are in your classroom.
b ☐ Say where things are in your classroom.
c ☐ Ask where places are in your school.
d ☐ Say where places are in your school.

What are the people saying?

Do it yourself.

೫ೱೱೱ MEMO ೫ೱೱೱ

TO: the teacher

Give students floor plans of the school with some rooms and other features unlabeled. Also give them a list of the places you want them to locate. Have students go out in pairs to fill in their floor plans. When they come back to the classroom, have them report where things are.

4 Community Services

Getting Started

1. Guess. What are Pablo and Han Fu saying?

2. What can you hear?

Conversations _____

1. Practice.

Han Fu: Look, Pablo! A fire!
Pablo: Oh, no! Call the fire department!
Han Fu: What's the phone number?
Pablo: 911.
Han Fu: There's a phone on the corner.
Pablo: Hurry, Han Fu!
         There are people in the building.

2. What can you say?

the fire department   an ambulance   the police

a fire   an accident   a robbery

3. Focus on grammar.

a	phone robbery	an	ambulance accident

4. Talk about an emergency. Use the words in 2. Use your partner's name.

A: Look, ___Pablo___ ! ___A fire___ !

B: Oh, no! Call ___the fire department___ !

A: What's the phone number?

B: ___911___ . Hurry!

Conversations

5. Practice.

Operator:	Emergency Services.
Han Fu:	Is this 911?
Operator:	Yes. What's the emergency?
Han Fu:	A fire!
Operator:	Where?
Han Fu:	At 302 First Avenue.
Operator:	What apartment?
Han Fu:	Oh! I don't know.
Operator:	What floor?
Han Fu:	It's on the second floor.

6. What can you say?

1st	2nd	3rd	4th	5th	6th	7th	8th	9th
first	second	third	fourth	fifth	sixth	seventh	eighth	ninth

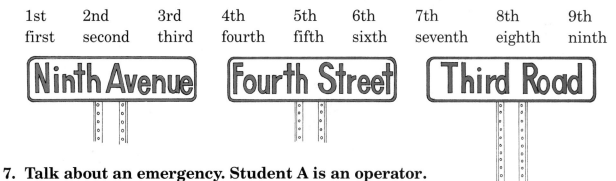

Ninth Avenue   Fourth Street   Third Road

7. Talk about an emergency. Student A is an operator.

A: 911. What's the emergency?

B: ___An accident___!

A: Where?

B: At ___529 First Avenue___.

A: What apartment?

B: In ___Apartment 9D___.

529 First Avenue
Apartment 9D

96 Seventh Street
Apartment 12

874 Second Road
Apartment F

Conversations

8. Practice.

Operator: OK. That's 302 First Avenue, second floor.
Han Fu: Right.
Operator: Is that between State and Main Streets?
Han Fu: Yes.
Operator: OK. Where are you?
Han Fu: On the corner of State Street and First Avenue.
Operator: What's the phone number?
Han Fu: It's 935-8531.

9. What can you say?

10. Focus on grammar.

The building is	on	Seventh Avenue.
	on the corner of	State Street and Seventh Avenue.
	between	Main and State Streets.

11. Talk about locations. Use the map in 9.

A: Where's the ___post office___?

B: On ___Seventh Avenue between Main and State Streets___.

A: ___Seventh Avenue between Main and State Streets___?

B: Right.

a. the post office   b. the fire department   c. the phone
d. the fire fighter   e. the mailbox   f. the police station
g. the library   h. the police officer   i. the hospital

Listening Plus _____

1. Say . . . Repeat . . . Point.

                       five hundred   eleven hundred

100   200   300   400   500   600   700   800   900   1000   1100

one hundred   one thousand
a hundred   a thousand

2. Say . . . Repeat . . . Point.

    a.   200 Eighth Avenue   b.   100 Fourth Street   c.   700 First Avenue

    d.   1100 Fifth Street   e.   5400 Second Avenue   f.   800 Seventh Street

3. Say . . . Repeat . . . Point.

    a.   576 Third Avenue   b.   438 Ninth Street   c.   59 Sixth Avenue

    d.   6212 First Street   e.   1328 Fifth Avenue   f.   1015 Eighth Street

4. Check what you hear. Use the addresses in 2 and 3.

5. Write the numbers you hear.

    a. __67__   b. _____   c. _____   d. _____   e. _____

    f. _____   g. _____   h. _____   i. _____   j. _____

Paperwork

1. Practice.

Sara: Anna, who can we call in an emergency?
Anna: Oh! Call my mother.
Sara: What's her name?
Anna: Kristina Kubiak.
Sara: How do you spell her last name?
Anna: It's K-U-B-I-A-K.
Sara: OK. And what's her address?
Anna: It's 91 West Street.
Sara: 91 West Street?
Anna: Yes. Apartment 7.
　　　Bridgeton, California.
Sara: OK. What's the ZIP code?
Anna: 93205.
Sara: And what's her phone number?
Anna: (209) 975-8134.

In case of emergency, notify:
Kristina Kubiak

Relation to you: mother

Address
91 West Street   7
Street   Apartment

Bridgeton,   California   93205
City   State   ZIP Code

Phone: (209) 975-8134

e

2. Fill in the form. Show your answers to a partner.

In case of emergency, notify:
_____

Relation to you: _____

Address:

Street   Apartment

City   State   ZIP Code

Phone: (_____) _____

f
g

3. Interview three classmates.
Write their information on a separate piece of paper.

Who can we call in an emergency?   mother

What's _her_ name?   Kristina Kubiak

What's _her_ address?   91 West Street
Bridgeton, California 93205

What's _her_ phone number?   (209) 975-8134

Reading and Writing _____

1. Focus on grammar.

There	is	a phone	on the corner.
	are	phones	

2. What can you say about the fire?

3. Read about the fire.

There is a fire at 302 First Avenue.
It's on the second floor.
It's in Apartment B.
There are people in Apartment A.
There are fire fighters next to the building.
There is a police officer on the corner.
There is an ambulance on Main Street between First and Second Avenues.

4. Match the questions with the answers.

Where is the fire?   On the corner.

Where are the fire fighters?   Next to the building.

Where is the police officer?   On the second floor.

Where are the people?   On Main Street.

Where is the ambulance?   In Apartment A.

Reading and Writing _____

5. On the map, write the names of streets in your community. Use real or imaginary information.

6. Draw these on your map:

    an accident   an ambulance   two police officers   people

7. Write about the accident. Fill in the blanks.

There is an accident _____

There is an ambulance _____

There are two police officers _____

There are people _____

8. Show your map to your group. Read your story to your group.

Interactions

Student A

1. Get information. Fill in the map. Ask about:

the school   the post office   the police station
the hospital   492 Fifth Street   Ray and David

A: Excuse me. Where __is the school__ ?

B: __It's on Post Avenue between Fifth Street and Sixth Street__ .

A: Thanks.

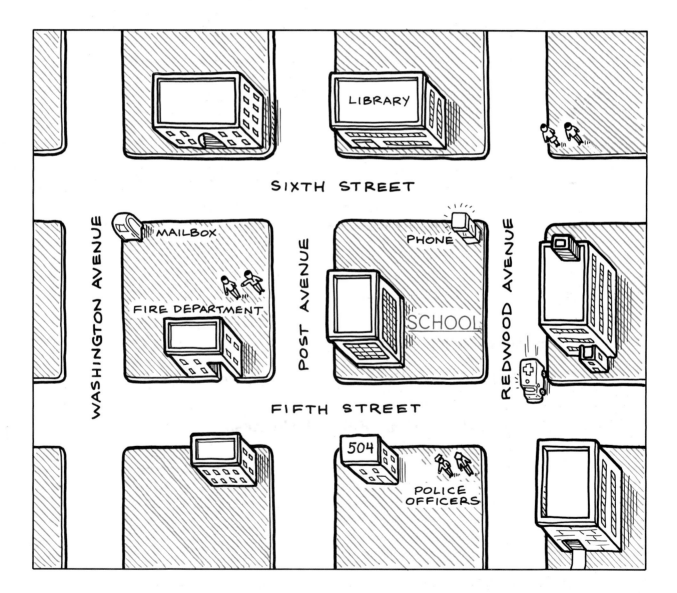

2. Give information about the map.

Interactions

Student B

1. Give information about the map.

A: Excuse me. Where ___is the school___ ?

B: ___It's on Post Avenue between Fifth Street and Sixth Street___ .

A: Thanks.

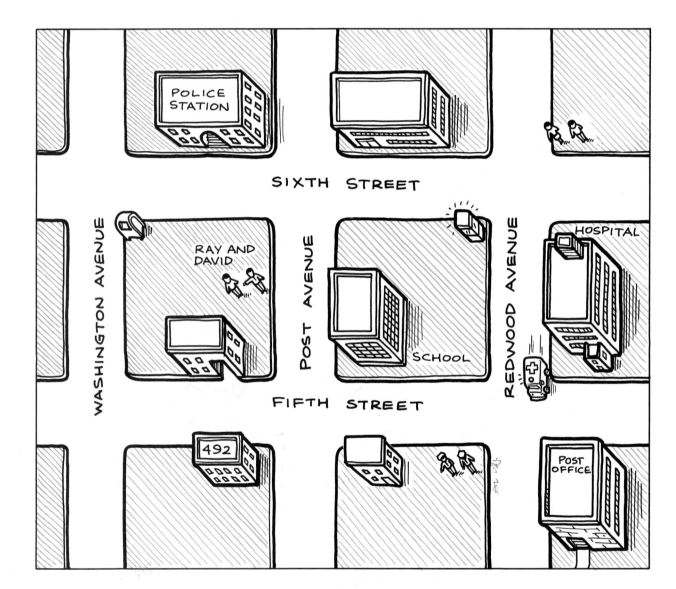

2. Get information. Fill in the map. Ask about:

the mailbox	the fire department	the phone
the library	504 Fifth Street	the police officers

Progress Checks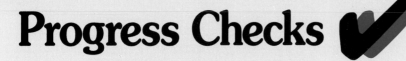

1. **e** ☐   Write your address.

   Fill in the form.

   Address: _____
                Number   Street   Apartment

   _____
                City   State   ZIP Code

2. **f** ☐   Ask for someone's address.
   g ☐   Give your address.

   What are the people saying?

   Do it yourself.

3. **a** ☐   Report an emergency.
   b ☐   Give the location of an emergency.

   What are the people saying?

   Do it yourself.

4. **c** ☐   Ask where places are in your community.
    d ☐   Give locations of places in your community.

What are the people saying?

Do it yourself.

೭ೱೱೱೱ MEMO ೭ೱೱೱೱ

TO: the teacher

Play "Emergency." Create a neighborhood using desks to represent city blocks and aisles to represent streets. Label streets and emergency services.

Team 1 puts team members at the fire department, the police station, and the hospital. Team 2 chooses an emergency and acts it out. Team 3 calls 911 (Team 1) to report the emergency. Team 1 responds to the scene.

Count the seconds from the beginning of Team 3's call to Team 1's arrival at the scene. Both teams get that number as their score (no score for Team 2 in this round). After several rounds, the lowest score wins.

5 Shopping

Getting Started _____

1. Guess. What are Rosa and Yuki saying?

2. What can you hear?

Conventions _____

1. Practice.

Yuki: Rosa!
Rosa: Hi, Yuki.
Yuki: Hi. What are you doing?
Rosa: I'm going to the drugstore.
    What about you?
Yuki: I'm going to the bank.
Rosa: Are you in a hurry?
Yuki: No.
Rosa: Good. Let's go to the drugstore together.
Yuki: OK.

2. What can you say?

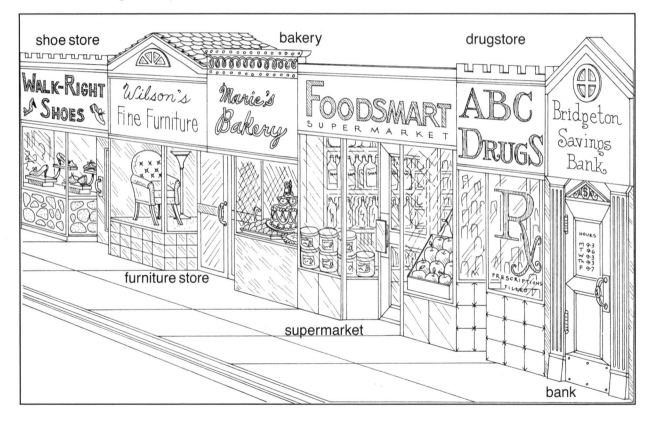

3. Talk about shopping. Use the stores in 2.

A: What are you doing?

B: I'm going to the ___drugstore___ .

    What about you?

A: I'm going to the ___bank___ .

Conversations _____

4. Practice.

Yuki: Are you ready?
Rosa: No. I'm waiting for my prescription.
           What are you doing?
Yuki: I'm looking for tissues.
           Excuse me. Where are the tissues?
Cashier: Tissues? Aisle 2.
Yuki: Thanks.

5. Focus on grammar.

What	are	you	doing?
	is	he	
		she	

I'm	looking for tissues.
He's	
She's	

6. What can you say?

7. Talk about locations in a store. Use the words in 6.

A: What are you doing?

B: I'm looking for _tissues_____.

     Excuse me. Where _are the tissues_____?

C: _Tissues_____? Aisle _2___.

B: Thanks.

Conversations _____

8. What can you say?

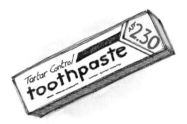

a. 89 cents

b. 1 dollar and 19 cents

c. 2 dollars and 30 cents

d. 1 dollar and 65 cents

e. 2 dollars and 89 cents

9. Practice.

Rosa:	ABC brand razor blades, please.
Cashier:	These?
Rosa:	Yes. How much are they?
Cashier:	They're $4.59.
Rosa:	That's a good price.
	How much are the batteries?
Cashier:	They're $3.19.
Rosa:	That's expensive.
	Just the razor blades, please.

10. Focus on grammar.

How much	is the aspirin? are the Band-Aids?

It's They're	$3.49.

11. Talk about prices. Use the items in 8.

A: How much <u>is the aspirin</u>?

B: <u>It's $1.65</u>.

A: That's expensive.   OR   That's a good price.

Listening Plus _____

1. Say . . . Repeat . . . Point.

1¢
one cent
a penny

5¢
five cents
a nickel

10¢
ten cents
a dime

25¢
twenty-five cents
a quarter

$1
one dollar
a dollar bill
a one-dollar bill

$5
five dollars
a five-dollar bill

$10
ten dollars
a ten-dollar bill

$20
twenty dollars
a twenty-dollar bill

2. Say . . . Repeat . . . Point.

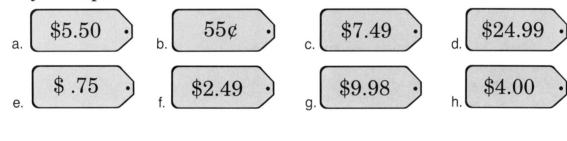

a. $5.50   b. 55¢   c. $7.49   d. $24.99

e. $ .75   f. $2.49   g. $9.98   h. $4.00

3. Write the prices you hear.

a. $5.50   b. _____   c. _____   d. _____

e. _____   f. _____   g. _____   h. _____

4. Check what you hear. Use the prices in 3.

What's the total?

It's five dollars and fifty cents.

Excuse me. How much?

Five dollars and fifty cents.

Paperwork _____

1. Practice.

Pablo: Hi, Sara. Are you busy?
Sara: No. What's up?
Pablo: I'm buying a picture dictionary.
Is this order form OK?
Sara: Hmmm. How are you paying?
With a check or a money order?
Pablo: With a money order.
Sara: OK. I'm putting an X in this box.
And the total is $6.50.
Now it's fine.
Pablo: Thanks, Sara.
Sara: You're welcome.

Method of payment: ☐ Check ☒ Money Order

Total enclosed: $ _6.50_

Name
Pablo Burgos
Address
1516 Union Street   _12_
                       Apartment No.
Bridgeton, California   _93205_
                       ZIP Code

2. Order something. Fill in the form.

Method of payment: ☐ Check ☐ Money Order

Total enclosed: $_____

Name

_____

Address

_____
                        Apartment No.

_____
                        ZIP Code

3. Interview three classmates.
Write their answers on a separate piece of paper.

What are you buying? _a picture dictionary_

What's the total? _$6.50_

How are you paying? _money order_

Reading and Writing _____

1. Match the sentences with the pictures.

She's waiting for her money.

Paula is going to the drugstore.

She's buying shampoo, aspirin, and Band-Aids.

She's paying for her prescription.

She's looking for shampoo.

2. Write the sentences in the correct order.

Paula is going to the drugstore. _____

_____

_____

_____

_____

Reading and Writing _____

3. **What can you say about the prices at these two drugstores?**

4. **Fill in the chart. Circle the good prices.**

	ABC Drugs	Main Street Pharmacy
aspirin	$2.09	$2.39
Band-Aids		
cold medicine		
razor blades		
shampoo		
toothpaste		

Interactions _____

Student A

1. **Get information about prices. Write the prices.**

    A: Excuse me.

    B: Yes. Can I help you?

    A: How much <u>is the toothpaste</u>?

    B: <u>It's $2.39</u>.

    A: <u>$2.39</u>? Thanks.

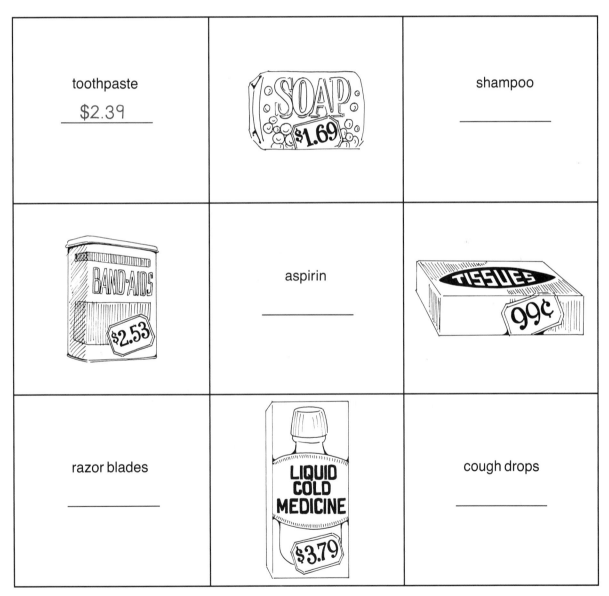

toothpaste <u>$2.39</u>	SOAP $1.69	shampoo _____
BAND-AIDS $2.53	aspirin _____	TISSUES 99¢
razor blades _____	LIQUID COLD MEDICINE $3.79	cough drops _____

2. **Give information about prices.**

Interactions

Student B

1. **Give information about prices.**

   A: Excuse me.

   B: Yes. Can I help you?

   A: How much <u>is the toothpaste</u>?

   B: <u>It's $2.39</u>.

   A: <u>$2.39</u>? Thanks.

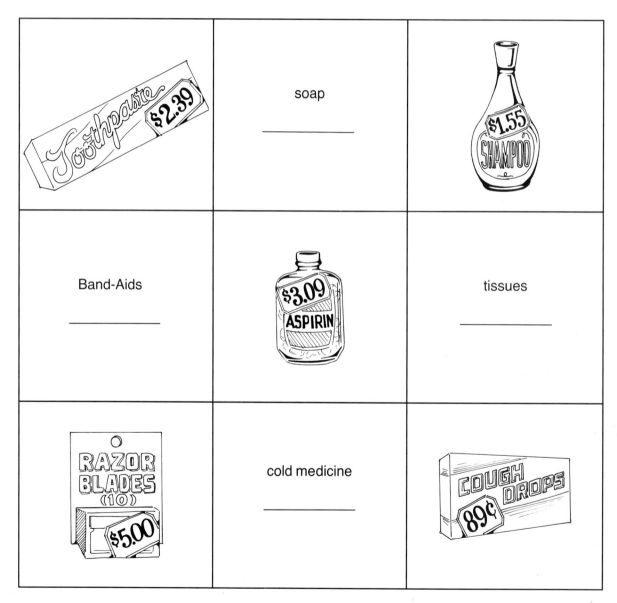

Toothpaste $2.39	soap _____	SHAMPOO $1.55
Band-Aids _____	ASPIRIN $3.09	tissues _____
RAZOR BLADES (10) $5.00	cold medicine _____	COUGH DROPS 89¢

2. **Get information about prices. Write the prices.**

Progress Checks

1. **e** ☐ Identify bills and coins.

Match the pictures and the words.

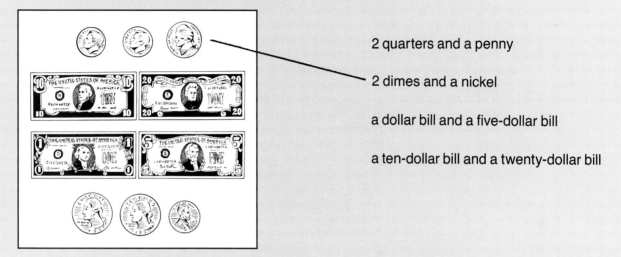

2 quarters and a penny

2 dimes and a nickel

a dollar bill and a five-dollar bill

a ten-dollar bill and a twenty-dollar bill

2. **a** ☐ Ask where things are in a store.
   b ☐ Read aisle numbers.

What are the people saying?

Do it yourself.

Progress Checks

3. c ☐ Ask for prices.
   d ☐ Read prices.
   f ☐ Ask for the total.

What are the people saying?

Do it yourself.

ჭჭჭჭ MEMO ჭჭჭჭ

TO: the teacher

Bring in various drugstore items. Set up shop using desks to represent shelves, aisles, and check-out counters. Have students label the aisles, put price tags on the items, and stock the shelves. Distribute play money or have students make their own. Supply calculators for cash registers if possible.

   Let students choose roles (shoppers, cashiers, pharmacists, store manager, stock clerks) and interact as much as they can.

6 Housing

Getting Started

1. Guess. What are Marie and Mrs. Edwards saying?

2. What can you hear?

Conventions _____

1. Practice.

Mrs. Edwards:	Hello.
Marie:	Hello. This is Marie Duval.
	I'm in Apartment 5A.
	May I speak to the manager?
Mrs. Edwards:	I'm sorry, he's not here.
	He's fixing the sink in Apartment 2C.
	Can I take a message?
Marie:	Yes, please. The stove isn't working.

2. What can you say?

stove

sink

shower

toilet

doorbell

refrigerator

**3. Talk about problems in a house. Use the words in 2.
Use any name and apartment number.**

A: Hello.

B: Hello. This is _Marie Duval_.

I'm in Apartment _5A_.

May I speak to the manager?

A: I'm sorry, he's not here.

Can I take a message?

B: Yes, please. The _stove_ isn't working.

Conversations

4. What can you say?

lights

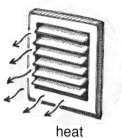

heat

gas

5. Practice.

Marie:	Who is it?
Mr. Edwards:	It's John Edwards, the manager.
Marie:	Hello, Mr. Edwards. Come in, please.
Mr. Edwards:	What's the problem?
Marie:	The stove isn't working.
Mr. Edwards:	Are the lights working?
Marie:	I don't know. Just a minute.
	No. The lights aren't working.

6. Focus on grammar.

is not	=	isn't
are not	=	aren't

7. Talk about a problem in the house. Use your name. Use the words in 4.

A: Who is it?

B: It's __John__ ___Edwards___, the manager.

A: Come in, please.

B: What's the problem?

A: The __lights__ __aren't__ working.

Unit 6

63

Conversations _____

8. Practice.

Marie: Hello.
Carmen: Hi, Marie. This is Carmen.
Marie: Hi, Carmen.
Carmen: Is your stove working now?
Marie: Yes, it is.
Carmen: That's good.
           Are you eating dinner?
Marie: No, I'm not. I'm cooking.

9. Focus on grammar.

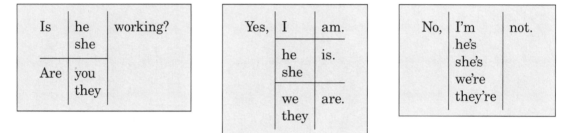

Is	he she	working?
Are	you they	

Yes,	I	am.
	he she	is.
	we they	are.

No,	I'm	not.
	he's she's we're they're	

10. Talk about the people.

A: <u> Is he eating dinner   </u>?

B: No, <u> he's </u> not.

    <u>He's cooking dinner   </u>.

eating dinner?

buying toothpaste?

going to the bank?

taking a message?

waiting for dinner?

fixing the stove?

Listening Plus

1. Say . . . Repeat . . . Point.

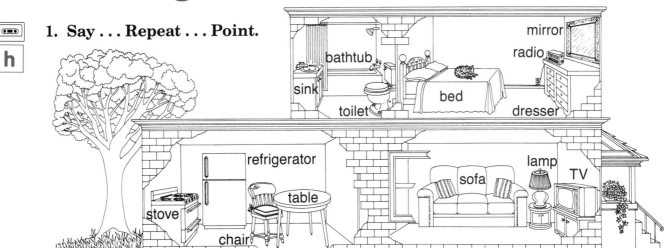

2. Write the word you hear.

a. <u>bed</u>　　　　b. _____　　　　c. _____

d. _____　　e. _____　　f. _____

g. _____　　h. _____

3. Check what you hear. Use the words in 2.

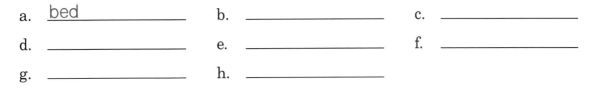

4. Say . . . Repeat . . . Point.

5. Write the word you hear.

a. <u>living room</u>　　　　　　b. _____

c. _____　　　　　　d. _____

Paperwork _____

1. Practice.

Sara: Westside Community Adult School.
        Sara Gilbert speaking.
Mary: Hello. My name is Mary Kim.
        I'm not coming to class today.
Sara: What's the problem?
Mary: The lights aren't working.
        I'm waiting for my landlord.
Sara: I see. What class are you in?
Mary: I'm in Level 2.
Sara: Who's your teacher?
Mary: Carl Walker.
Sara: OK, Mary. Thanks for calling.

WHILE YOU WERE OUT

To: _____ Carl Walker _____

From: _____ Mary Kim _____

Message: _____

_____

_____

2. Write Mary's message for Carl.

WHILE YOU WERE OUT

To: _____

From: _____

Message: _____

_____

_____

3. Use your imagination. Three classmates are not coming to school today. Take three messages.

What's your name, please? _____ Mary Kim _____

What class are you in? _____ Level 2 _____

Who's your teacher? _____ Carl Walker _____

What's the problem? _____ The lights aren't working. _____

Reading and Writing _____

1. What can you say about Marie's family?

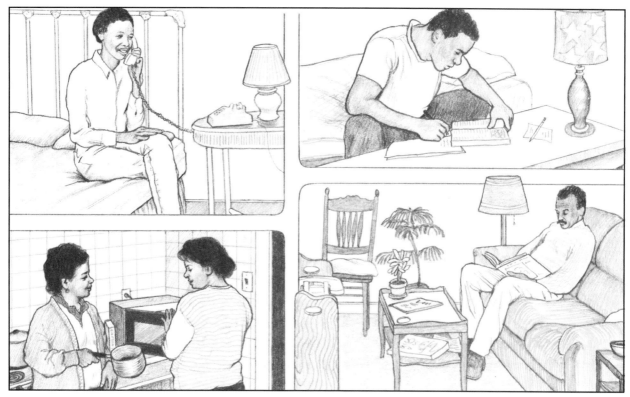

2. Read about Marie and her family.

Marie is in the bedroom.
She's calling her mother.
Her husband, Claude, is in the living room.
He's reading a book.
Their son, Paul, is in his bedroom.
He's studying English.
Their daughters, Martine and Eve, are cooking dinner.

3. Fill in the chart.

Name	Relationship to Marie	Where	What/doing
Marie	—		
Claude		living room	
Paul			
Martine and Eve			cooking dinner

Reading and Writing _____

4. **Draw a floor plan of your home.**
   Draw your family or friends in the picture.

5. **Fill in the form about your family or friends in 4.**

Name	Relationship to you	Where	What/doing

6. **Write about your picture. Use the information in 5.**

_____

_____

_____

_____

_____

7. **Read your story to your group.**

Interactions

Student A

1. **Get information. Write the messages.**

   A: Hello.

   B: Hello. This is _____.

   May I speak to the manager?

   A: I'm sorry, he's busy.

   Can I take a message?

   B: Yes. I'm in Apartment __7H__.

   The __refrigerator isn't__ working.

   A: Apartment __7H__.

   The __refrigerator isn't__ working.

2. **Give information. Use any name.**

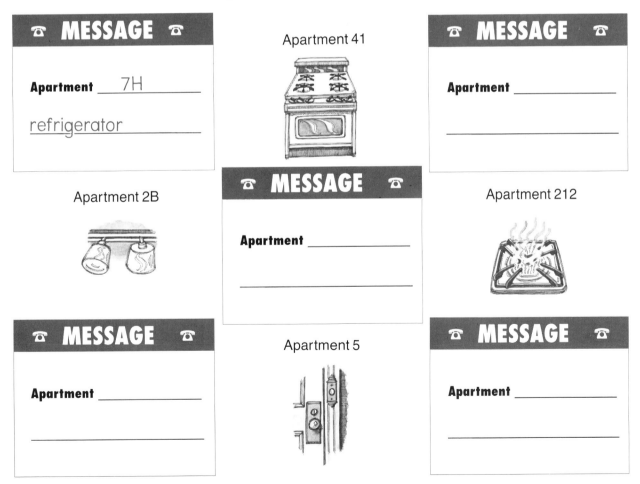

☎ **MESSAGE** ☎

Apartment __7H__

refrigerator

Apartment 41

☎ **MESSAGE** ☎

Apartment _____

_____

Apartment 2B

☎ **MESSAGE** ☎

Apartment _____

_____

Apartment 212

☎ **MESSAGE** ☎

Apartment _____

_____

Apartment 5

☎ **MESSAGE** ☎

Apartment _____

_____

Interactions _____

Student B

1. Give information. Use any name.

A: Hello.

B: Hello. This is _____.

   May I speak to the manager?

A: I'm sorry, he's busy.

   Can I take a message?

B: Yes. I'm in Apartment __7H__.

   The __refrigerator isn't__ working.

A: Apartment __7H__.

   The __refrigerator isn't__ working.

2. Get information. Write the messages.

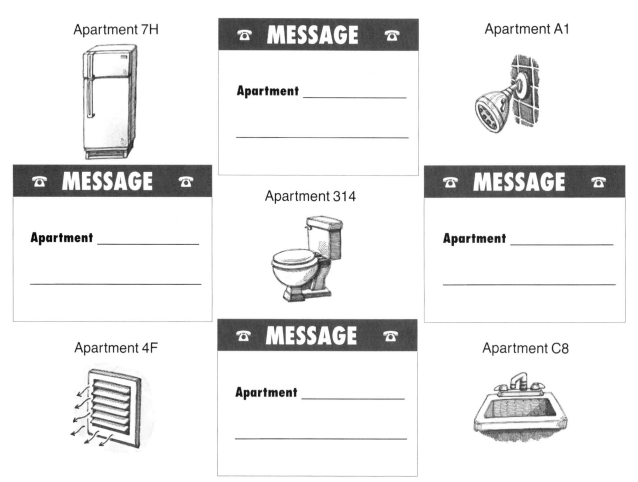

Apartment 7H

☎ **MESSAGE** ☎

Apartment _____

_____

Apartment A1

☎ **MESSAGE** ☎

Apartment _____

_____

Apartment 314

☎ **MESSAGE** ☎

Apartment _____

_____

Apartment 4F

☎ **MESSAGE** ☎

Apartment _____

_____

Apartment C8

Progress Checks

1. **e** ☐ Ask "Who is it?" when someone is at the door.
    f ☐ Answer the question, "Who is it?"
    g ☐ Report problems in a house.

What are the people saying?

Do it yourself.

2. **h** ☐ Name furniture in a house.
    i ☐ Name rooms in a house.

Talk to your partner. Name the rooms. Name the furniture.

Progress Checks

3. **a** ☐   Answer the phone.
     b ☐   Give your name on the phone.
     c ☐   Ask for someone on the phone.
     d ☐   Say that someone is not here.

What are the people saying?

Do it yourself. Ask for a friend.

⁔⁔⁔⁔ MEMO ⁔⁔⁔⁔

TO: the teacher

Have students work in groups to design a "dream house." They can draw pictures and make floor plans together. Then they can go to "stores" around the classroom to buy pictures, furniture, and appliances (simple drawings or magazine cutouts). When they finish, they can show their house to another group and tell them about the rooms and the furniture.

7 Recreation

Getting Started

1. Guess. What are Victor and Trong saying?

2. What can you hear?

Conversations

1. Practice.

1. Practice.

Victor: Trong, do you want to come over on Friday?
Trong: Sure. Oh wait.
         I'm sorry. I'm busy on Friday.
Victor: How about Saturday?
         Are you free?
Trong: Yes, I am. Saturday is fine.

2. What can you say?

come over

go to the park

go to the movies

watch TV

play cards

3. Talk about the activities in 2.

A: Do you want to __come over__ on Saturday?

B: Sure.

4. What can you say?

Sunday	Monday	Tuesday	Wednesday	Thursday	Friday	Saturday

Conversations

C

5. Talk about plans. Use the days of the week in 4.

A: Do you want to __play cards__ on __Saturday__?

B: I'm sorry. I'm busy on __Saturday__.

A: How about __Sunday__? Are you free?

B: Yes, I am. __Sunday__ is fine.

6. Practice.

Victor: Do you know my address?
Trong: No, I don't. What is it?
Victor: It's 310 Fourth Avenue, Apartment 5G.
Trong: OK. What time?
Victor: 6:30. Do you have a car?
Trong: Yes, I do.
Victor: Do you need directions?
Trong: No, I don't. I have a map.

7. Focus on grammar.

Do you	know have need	my address?

Yes, I do.
No, I don't.

8. Talk about yourself.

A: Do you __have a car__?

B: Yes, I do.   OR   No, I don't.

a. have a car   b. know my phone number   c. need my address
d. know my last name   e. have a daughter   f. need a map

Conversations _____

9. What can you say?

morning   afternoon   evening   night

10. Practice.

Victor: How's your new job, Trong?
Trong: It's fine.
Victor: Do you work on Monday?
Trong: I work on Monday afternoon.
       I don't work on Monday morning.

11. What can you say?

do the laundry   go to school   clean the house   visit my family

12. Focus on grammar.

I	(don't)	work on Monday morning.
You		
We		
They		

13. Talk about yourself. Use the activities in 11. Use any days and any times.

A: Do you ___do the laundry___ on ___Saturday___ ___morning___ ?

B: Yes. I do.

OR

No. I don't. I ___do the laundry___ on ___Monday___ ___night___.

OR

I don't ___do the laundry___.

Listening Plus

1. Say ... Repeat ... Point.

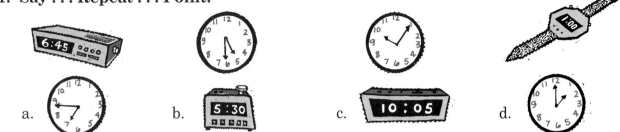

a.　　　　b.　　　　c.　　　　d.

2. Say ... Repeat ... Point.

f g

3. Check what you hear. Use the times in 2.

4. Write the times you hear.

a. _8_ : 1 5　　　b. 2 : __ __　　　c. 9 : __ __　　　d. 1 2 : __ __

e. __ : __ __　　　f. __ : __ __　　　g. __ : __ __　　　h. __ : __ __

Paperwork _____

1. Practice.

Neary: Hi, Sara. Can you help me?
Sara: Sure, Neary. What can I do for you?
Neary: Here, look. What is <u>employed</u>?
Sara: Employed. Are you <u>employed</u>?
       Do you have a job?
Neary: Oh. Yes, I do.
       And what's <u>SSN</u>?
Sara: That's Social Security number.
       Do you have a Social Security card?
Neary: Yes, I do.
Sara: Do you know your Social Security number?
Neary: Yes. Just a minute. It's 589-47-6132.

Name:

Som	Neary
Last	First

Employed: (circle one) (Yes) No

SSN: _589 – 47 – 6132_

h   **2. Fill in the form.**

Name: _____

_____
Last   First

Employed: (circle one) Yes   No

SSN: _____ – _____ – _____

3. Interview three classmates.
Write their information on a separate piece of paper.

Do you have a job? _____yes_____

Do you have a Social Security card? _____yes_____

Do you know your Social Security number? ___589-47-6132_____

Reading and Writing _____

1. Look at Neary's schedule.

	SUNDAY	MONDAY	TUESDAY
morning	visit my family	go to school	go to school
afternoon	visit my family	work	go to the supermarket
evening	go to the movies		
night		watch TV	

2. Read Neary's story.

On Sunday, I visit my family.
On Sunday evening, I go to the movies.
On Monday and Tuesday mornings, I go to school.
On Monday afternoon, I work.
On Monday and Tuesday evenings, I'm free.
On Monday night, I watch TV.
On Tuesday afternoon, I go to the supermarket.

3. Match.

Sunday evening   go to school

Monday night   go to the movies

Tuesday morning   work

Monday afternoon   watch TV

Reading and Writing _____

4. Fill in your schedule. Use these words or other words you know.

go to school   go to the park   watch TV   play cards   work

clean the house   go to the movies   do the laundry   visit my family

	THURSDAY	**FRIDAY**	**SATURDAY**
morning			
afternoon			
evening			
night			

5. Write about your schedule. Fill in the blanks.
Use Neary's story as an example.

On Thursday _____ , I _____

On Thursday _____ , I _____

On Friday _____ , I _____

On Friday _____ , I _____

On Saturday _____ , I _____

On Saturday _____ , I _____

6. Read your story to your group.

Interactions

Student A

1. **Give and get information. When are you and Student B free?**

   A: Do you want to <u>come over on Friday morning</u> ?

   B: I'm sorry. I'm busy.

       I <u>go to school on Friday morning</u> .

       How about <u>Friday afternoon</u> ?

   A: _____

This is your schedule.

	FRIDAY	SATURDAY	SUNDAY
morning			
afternoon	watch TV	clean the house	
evening			visit my family
night	work	play cards	visit my family

Interactions _____

Student B

1. Give and get information. When are you and Student A free?

A: Do you want to <u>come over on Friday morning</u>?

B: I'm sorry. I'm busy.

    I <u>go to school on Friday morning</u>.

    How about <u>Friday afternoon</u>?

A: _____

This is your schedule.

	FRIDAY	SATURDAY	SUNDAY
morning	go to school	work	do the laundry
afternoon			
evening	go to the movies	visit my family	play cards
night			watch TV

Progress Checks

1. **h** ☐   Write your Social Security number.

Fill in the form.

Name: _____
      Last   First   MI

SSN: _____

2. **f** ☐   Ask the time.
   g ☐   Tell someone the time.

What are the people saying?

Do it yourself.

3. **d** ☐   Ask about someone's weekly activities.
   e ☐   State your weekly activities.

What are the people saying?

Do it yourself.

Progress Checks

4. **a** ☐ Invite someone to do something.
   b ☐ Respond to an invitation.
   c ☐ Set a day to do something with someone.

What are the people saying?

Do it yourself.

ᔥᔥᔥ MEMO ᔥᔥᔥ

TO: the teacher

Give each student a week from a datebook. Students choose three things to do with a friend (go to the movies, play cards) and fill in three days in the datebook. Then students try to find companions who are free on the right days. Students should also accept invitations for the days when they are free and fill in the datebook with names and plans.

8 Health

Getting Started _____

1. Guess. What are Anna and Mrs. Webb saying?

2. What can you hear?

Conversations

1. Practice.

Mrs. Webb: Hello. May I help you?
Anna: Yes. My name is Anna Skalska.
            I'm here with my son, Eddie.
Mrs. Webb: What's the matter?
Anna: He feels sick.
Mrs. Webb: Oh. That's too bad.

2. What can you say?

sick   dizzy   nauseous   tired

3. Practice.

Mrs. Webb: Does he feel nauseous?
Anna: Yes, he does.
Mrs. Webb: Does he feel dizzy?
Anna: No, he doesn't.

4. Focus on grammar.

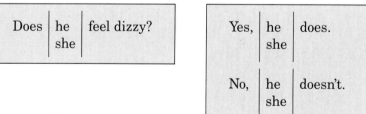

Does	he	feel dizzy?
	she	

Yes,	he	does.
	she	

No,	he	doesn't.
	she	

5. Talk about the woman. Use the words in 2.

A: Does she feel ___sick___?

B: ___Yes, she does___.

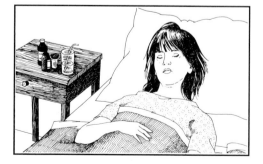

86   Unit 8

Conversations _____

6. What can you say?

a fever   a sore throat   a cold   a toothache

a headache   a stomachache   an earache   a backache

7. Practice.

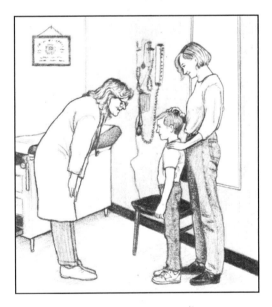

Dr. Kane:	Hello, Eddie.
	How are you?
Eddie:	I don't feel well, Doctor.
	My head hurts.
Dr. Kane:	Does he have a fever, Ms. Skalska?
Anna:	Yes. He has a fever and a headache.
Dr. Kane:	Does he have a sore throat?
Anna:	No. He doesn't have a sore throat.
	But he has a stomachache.

8. Focus on grammar.

He	has	a sore throat.
She	doesn't have	

a **9. Talk about Eddie.**

A: Does he have __a toothache__?

B: __No. He doesn't have a toothache__.

__He has a stomachache__.

No	*Yes*
a sore throat	a fever
a cold	a headache
a toothache	a stomachache
a backache	
an earache	

Conversations

10. What can you say?

Sit on the table.

Breathe in.

Breathe out.

Open your mouth.

Say Ah.

Roll up your sleeve.

11. Practice.

Dr. Kane: OK, Eddie. Sit on the table.
Eddie: Here?
Dr. Kane: Yes. Now breathe in.
                   Breathe out. Good.
                   Open your mouth.

12. Student A, give instructions. Student B, follow the instructions. Use the sentences in 10.

13. Practice.

Dr. Kane: OK, Eddie. You have the flu.
Anna: Does he need a prescription?
Dr. Kane: Yes. Here it is.
Anna: Thank you.
Dr. Kane: You're welcome. Goodbye, Eddie.
Eddie: Bye.

14. Say thank you and goodbye.

A: Here's your prescription.

B: Thank you.

A: You're welcome.

B: <u>Goodbye</u>.

A: <u>Bye</u>.

Listening Plus

1. Say . . . Repeat . . . Point.

2. Student A, say a part of the body. Student B, point.

3. Check what you hear. Use the words in 1.

4. Write the part of the body you hear.

a. _____chest_____   b. _____   c. _____

d. _____   e. _____   f. _____

g. _____   h. _____

Paperwork _____

1. Practice.

Mrs. Webb:	Excuse me, Ms. Skalska. I need more information. Is it Mrs., Miss, or Ms.?
Anna:	It's Ms. M-S.
Mrs. Webb:	And what's your middle initial?
Anna:	It's M. My middle name is Maria.
Mrs. Webb:	Do you have health insurance?
Anna:	No, I don't.
Mrs. Webb:	And your marital status?
Anna:	Marital status?
Mrs. Webb:	Are you single, married, separated, divorced, or widowed?
Anna:	Oh. I'm separated.

Title: *(Circle one)* Mr. Miss Mrs. (Ms.)

Name:

_Skalska_____ _Anna_____ _M._
Last   First   MI

Health Insurance: *(Circle one)* Yes (No)

Marital Status: *(Check one)*

☐ Single   ☐ Married   ☐ Widowed

☑ Separated   ☐ Divorced

---

2. Fill in the form.

Title: *(Circle one)* Mr. Miss Mrs. Ms.

Name:

_____
Last   First   MI

Health Insurance: *(Circle one)* Yes No

Marital Status: *(Check one)*

☐ Single   ☐ Married   ☐ Widowed

☐ Separated   ☐ Divorced

---

3. Interview three students.
Write their information on a separate piece of paper.

What's your name? ____Anna Skalska_____

What's your middle initial? _____M._____

What's your marital status? _____Separated_____

Do you have health insurance? _____No_____

Reading and Writing _____

1. What can you say about Sara?

2. Read Sara's story.

I feel sick.

I have a cold.

I have a sore throat.

I don't have a fever.

I feel tired.

My eyes hurt.

3. Write about Sara.

She feels sick.

_____

_____

_____

_____

_____

Reading and Writing _____

4. Fill in the blanks.

a. Does his arm hurt?

No, it doesn't.

His __stomach__ hurts.

b. _____ her head hurt?

No, _____ doesn't.

Her _____ _____

c. _____ her ear _____

No, _____ _____

_____ _____ _____

d. _____ _____ leg _____

No, _____ _____

_____ _____ _____

e. _____ _____ back _____

No, _____ _____

_____ _____ _____

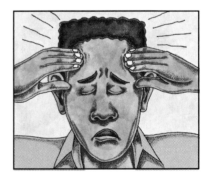

f. _____ _____ throat _____

No, _____ _____

_____ _____ _____

Interactions

Student A

1. **Give information. Talk about these health problems.**

   a. a cold   b. a headache   c. an earache

   d. a stomachache   e. a sore throat   f. a fever

   A: _Ed_ feels sick.

   B: Does _he_ have _a cold_ ?

   A: No. _He_ doesn't have _a cold_ .

   B: Does _he_ have _a headache_ ?

   A: Yes. _He_ has _a headache_ .

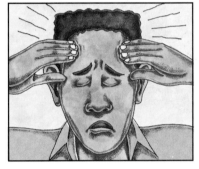

Ed

Marta

_____

Eve

Paul

_____

John

Silvia

_____

2. **Get information. Write the answer.**

Interactions

Student B

1. Get information. Write the answer.
Talk about these health problems.

a. a cold   b. a headache   c. an earache

d. a stomachache   e. a sore throat   f. a fever

A: ___Ed___ feels sick.

B: Does _he_ have ___a cold___?

A: No. _He_ doesn't have ___a cold___.

B: Does _he_ have ___a headache___?

A: Yes. _He_ has ___a headache___.

Ed

a headache

Marta

Eve

_____

Paul

John

_____

Silvia

2. Give information.

94   Unit 8

Progress Checks

1. **f** ☐ Write your name with your middle initial.
   g ☐ Show your marital status on a form.

   Fill in the form.

   ☐ **Mr.** ☐ **Ms.** ☐ **Mrs.** ☐ **Miss** _____

                                        Last   First   MI

   Marital Status: ☐ single ☐ married ☐ divorced ☐ separated ☐ widowed

2. **h** ☐ Give your marital status.

   What are the people saying?

   Do it yourself.

3. **a** ☐ Report health problems.
   e ☐ Name parts of your body.

   What are the people saying?

   Do it yourself.

Progress Checks

4. **b** ☐ Follow instructions in a medical examination.

Who is following instructions? Circle the picture.

5. **c** ☐ Say and respond to "Thank you."
   d ☐ Say and respond to "Goodbye."

What are the people saying?

Do it yourself.

୬୬୬୬୬ MEMO ୬୬୬୬୬

TO: the teacher

Set up a clinic in the classroom with a waiting room, examination rooms, and a dispensary. Students take the roles of patients, patients' family members, receptionists, nurses, doctors, and pharmacists. A student-generated list of questions on the board can facilitate interaction.

9 Transportation

Getting Started

1. Guess. What are Babacar and Victor saying?

2. What can you hear?

Conversations _____

1. Practice.

Babacar: Bye, Victor.
Victor: Wait, Babacar. Where are you going?
Babacar: I'm taking the train to Oakland.
Victor: Where do you get the train?
Babacar: At the train station near Union Park.
Victor: How do you get there?
Babacar: I take the bus.
Victor: When does your train leave?
Babacar: At 1:30.
Victor: Hurry, Babacar. You're late!

2. Focus on grammar.

How Where When	do	I you we they	go?
	does	he she it	

3. What can you say?

4. Talk about yourself. Use the words in 3.

A: Where are you going?

B: I'm going to __the supermarket__.

A: How do you get there?

B: I __walk__.

a. the supermarket
b. school
c. the hospital
d. my friend's house

Conversations

5. Practice.

Babacar: Excuse me.
Does this bus go to the train station?
Bus Driver: Yes, it does.
Babacar: Where do I get off?
Bus Driver: Get off at Union Street.

6. What can you say?

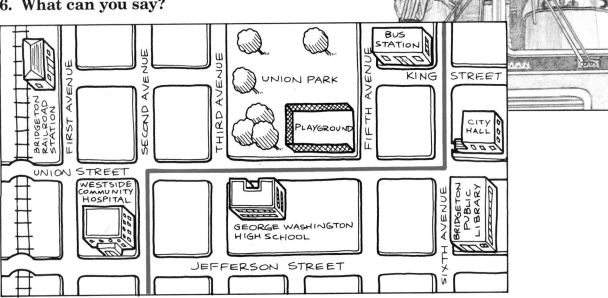

**7. Talk about buses. Use the conversation in 5.
Use the map and words in 6.**

8. Practice.

Woman: Does the VA Hospital bus stop here?
Bus Driver: No, it doesn't.
It stops at Third Avenue.
Woman: Thank you.

9. Talk about buses. Use the conversation in 8.

Conversations _____

10. What can you say?

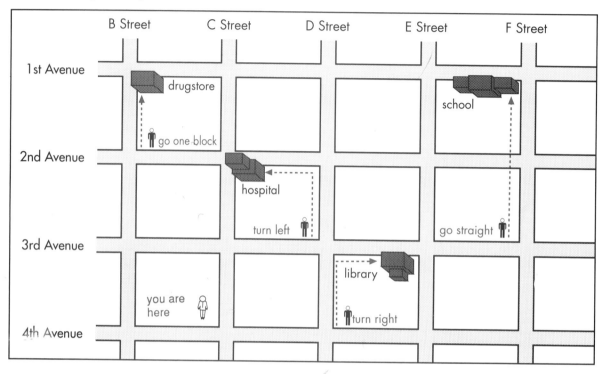

11. Practice.

Babacar: Excuse me. How do I get to the train station?
Man: Go straight on Union Street to First Avenue.
Turn right on First Avenue.
Then go one block.
Babacar: I go straight on Union Street.
I turn right on First Avenue.
Then I go one block.
Man: That's right.

12. Give directions. Use the conversation in 11. Use the map in 10.

Listening Plus _____

1. **Say . . . Repeat . . . Point.**

   11th 12th 13th 14th 15th 16th 17th 18th 19th

   10th 20th 30th 40th 50th 60th 70th 80th 90th

2. **Check what you hear. Point to the number in 1.**

3. **Say . . . Repeat . . . Point.**

   21st 22nd 23rd 24th 25th 26th 27th 28th 29th

4. **Write the number you hear.**

	1st	2nd	3rd	4th	5th	6th	7th	8th	9th
10th tenth									
20th twentieth									
30th thirtieth									
40th fortieth									
50th fiftieth									
60th sixtieth					65th				
70th seventieth									
80th eightieth									
90th ninetieth									

5. **Student A, say a number. Student B, write the number in the chart.**

Paperwork

1. Practice.

Yuki: Here's my questionnaire, Sara.
But I don't understand these three questions.
Sara: OK. Location of home.
Where do you live?
Yuki: On King Street.
Sara: Between?
Yuki: Between 11th Avenue and 12th Avenue.
Sara: How do you get to school?
Yuki: I take the bus.
On Friday, I get a ride with my sister.
Sara: OK. And when do you leave for school?
Yuki: At 8:30.

> **6. Location of home.**
> *(Give street and cross-streets.)*
>
> _King Street_
> Street
>
> _11th Avenue and 12th Avenue_
> Between
>
> **7. Transportation to school.**
> *(Check all that apply.)*
>
> ☐ walk ☑ bus ☐ drive
> ☑ other _ride_
>
> **8. Time you leave for school.** _8:30_

2. Fill in the form.

> **6. Location of home.**
> *(Give street and cross-streets.)*
>
> _____
> Street
>
> _____
> Between
>
> **7. Transportation to school.**
> *(Check all that apply.)*
>
> ☐ walk ☐ bus ☐ drive
>
> ☐ other _____
>
> **8. Time you leave for school.** _____

g **3. Interview three classmates. Use a separate piece of paper.**

Where do you live? _King Street between 11th Avenue and 12th Avenue_

How do you get to school? _take the bus_ _get a ride_

When do you leave for school? _8:30_

Reading and Writing _____

1. What can you say about Victor's route to school?

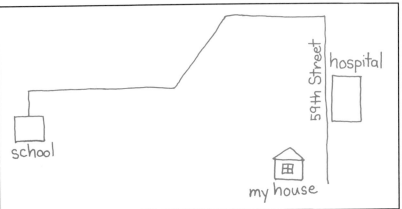

2. Read about Victor.

Victor goes to the Westside Community Adult School.
He doesn't live near school.
He lives on 59th Street near Bridgeton Community Hospital.
He drives to school.
He leaves for school at 8:10.
He gets to school at 8:45.
His class is at 9:00.

3. Answer the questions.

1. Where does Victor go to school?

   <u>Victor goes to the Westside Community Adult School.</u>

2. Does he live near school?

   _____

3. Where does he live?

   _____

4. How does he get to school?

   _____

5. When does he leave for school?

   _____

6. When does he get to school?

   _____

7. When is his class?

   _____

Reading and Writing _____

4. Draw your route to school. Use real or imaginary information.

5. Answer the questions.

1. Where do you go to school?

   _____

2. Do you live near school?

   _____

3. Where do you live?

   _____

4. How do you get to school?

   _____

5. When do you leave for school?

   _____

6. When do you get to school?

   _____

7. When is your class?

   _____

h **6. Show your map to your group. Read your story to your group.**

Interactions

Student A

i

1. **Get directions. Label the buildings.**

   Ask about: a. the clinic   b. the post office   c. Yuki's house

                        d. the supermarket   e. the police station   f. the library

   A: Excuse me. How do I get to <u> the clinic   </u>?

   B: <u>Go straight to 11th Avenue   </u>.

          <u>Turn left on 11th Avenue   </u>.

          <u>Go two blocks   </u>.

   A: Thanks.

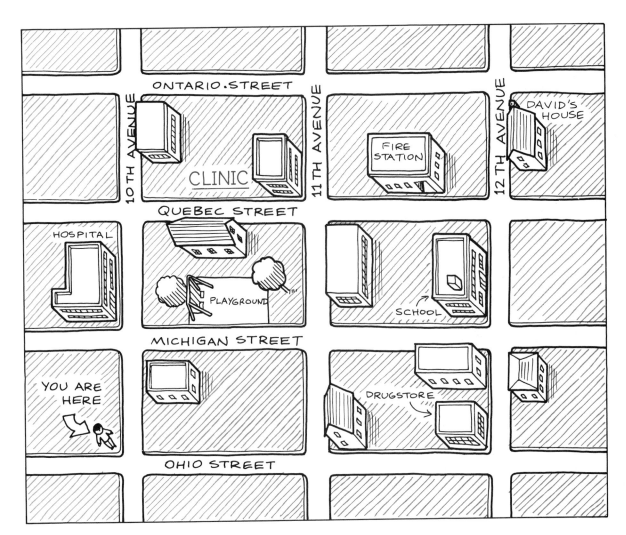

2. **Give directions.**

Interactions

Student B

1. Give directions. Label the buildings.

A: Excuse me. How do I get to __the clinic__?

B: __Go straight to 11th Avenue__.

__Turn left on 11th Avenue__.

__Go two blocks__.

A: Thanks.

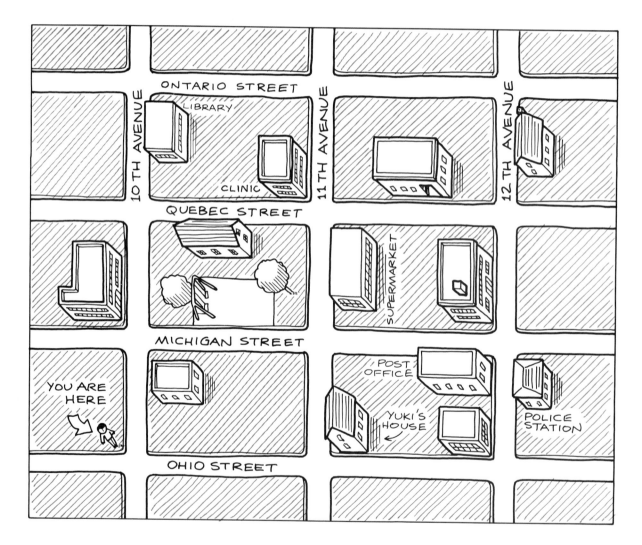

2. Get directions.

Ask about:
- a. the fire station
- b. the playground
- c. David's house
- d. the school
- e. the hospital
- f. the drugstore

Progress Checks

1. **g** ☐ Give the streets near your house.
   h ☐ Give a landmark near your house.

What are the people saying?

Do it yourself.

2. **b** ☐ Ask where the bus goes.
   d ☐ Read bus destination and street signs.
   a ☐ Say where you are going.
   c ☐ Ask where to get off the bus.

What are the people saying?

Do it yourself. Use the signs.

Progress Checks ✔

3. **e** ☐ Ask for directions.
   f ☐ Give directions.
   i ☐ Follow directions.

What are the people saying?

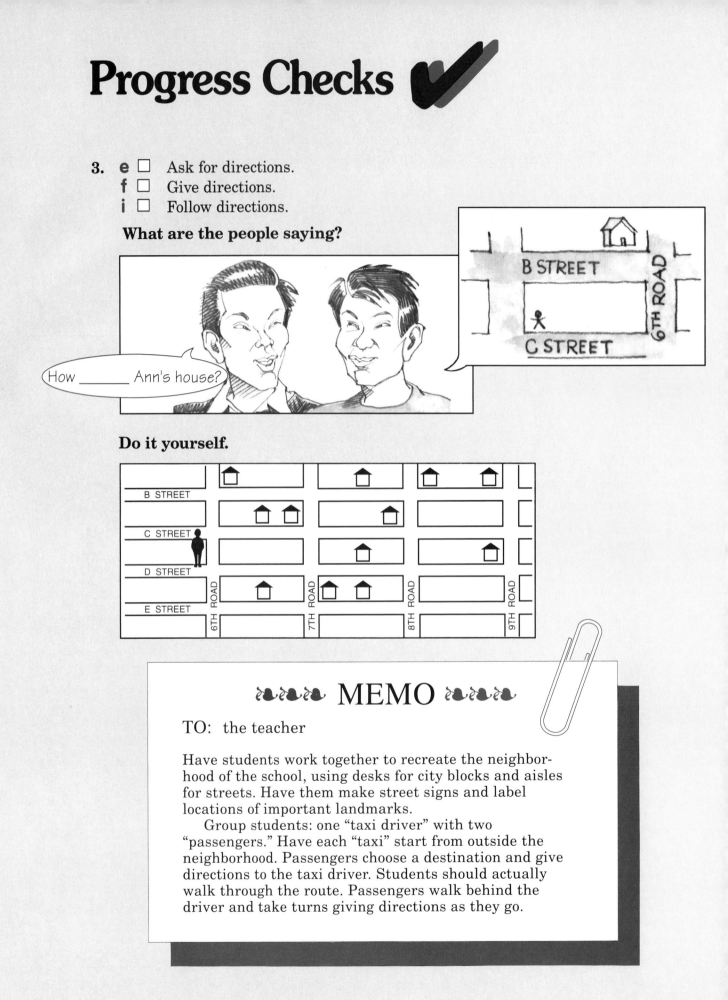

How _____ Ann's house?

Do it yourself.

৫৮৫৮৫৮ MEMO ৫৮৫৮৫৮

TO: the teacher

Have students work together to recreate the neighborhood of the school, using desks for city blocks and aisles for streets. Have them make street signs and label locations of important landmarks.

   Group students: one "taxi driver" with two "passengers." Have each "taxi" start from outside the neighborhood. Passengers choose a destination and give directions to the taxi driver. Students should actually walk through the route. Passengers walk behind the driver and take turns giving directions as they go.

10 Employment

Getting Started

1. **Guess. What are Carrie and Carmen saying?**

2. **What can you hear?**

Conversations _____

1. Practice.

Carmen: Hi, Carrie.
Carrie: Hi, Carmen.
　　　　Carmen, wait! Don't use the time clock.
Carmen: What's wrong?
Carrie: It isn't working.
Carmen: OK. See you.
Carrie: Wait! Don't go.
　　　　First fill out this time sheet.

2. What can you say?

3. Focus on grammar.

Don't	use the time clock.
	go.

4. Warn your partner.

A: Wait!

B: What's wrong?

A: It says ___Danger___ .

　　Don't ___open the door___ .

a. Danger	b. Keep Out	c. No Smoking	d. Out of Order
open the door	go in there	smoke here	use the washing machine

Conversations _____

5. Practice.

Carmen: Carrie, can you help me?
I don't know how to fill out the time sheet.
Carrie: OK. No problem.
Carmen: And can I use your pen?
Carrie: Sure. Here you are.

6. What can you say?

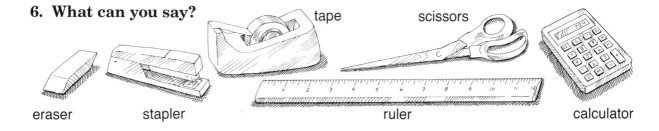

eraser   stapler   tape   scissors   ruler   calculator

b

7. Talk about things at work. Use the words in 6.

A: Excuse me. Can I use your _____eraser_____?

B: My _____eraser_____?

Sure. Here you are.

A: Thanks.

8. Practice.

Carrie: Write your name here.
Carmen: Do I print or sign?
Carrie: Print.
Carmen: Is this right?
Carrie: Yes.

C.J. Roberts and Company				Time Sheet	
Employee's Name (please print) Soto _____ Last				Carmen _____ First	
Job Title _____					
Date	**In**	**Out**	**In**	**Out**	**Total**
					Weekly Total
Signature _____					

9. Talk about yourself. Use the conversation in 8.

C.J. Roberts and Company   **Time Sheet**

Employee's Name (please print) _____   _____
                                Last   First

Job Title _____

Date	**In**	**Out**	**In**	**Out**	**Total**

Conversations _____

10. Practice.

Carrie: Write your job title here.
Carmen: My job title?
Carrie: Yes. What do you do?
Carmen: Oh. I'm a machine operator.

11. What can you say?

a homemaker   a mechanic   a cook   a carpenter   a machine operator

c d

12. Talk about jobs. Use the jobs in 11.

A: What do you do?

B: I'm a ___homemaker___. And you?

A: I'm a ___mechanic___.

13. Practice.

Carrie: Write today's date on this line.
Carmen: What's today's date?
Carrie: It's February 8.
Now write the time here.
Carmen: Thanks.

C.J. Roberts and Company   **Time Sheet**

Employee's Name (please print) Soto   Carmen
                                Last   First
Job Title machine operator

Date	In	Out	In	Out	Total
2/8/92	1:00				

Signature   **Weekly Total**

e

14. Talk about yourself. Use the conversations in 10 and 13.

Job Title _____

Date	In	Out	In	Out	Total

Listening Plus

1. Say . . . Repeat . . . Point.

January 1	February 14	March 17	April 15	May 30
June 21	July 4	August 22	September 3	
October 31	November 11	December 25		

f **2. Check what you hear. Use the dates in 1.**

3. Say . . . Repeat . . . Point.

1984   1776   1492   2001   1959   1812

4. Write the date you hear.

g

a. _October 18, 1932_   b. _____

c. _____   d. _____

e. _____   f. _____

g. _____   h. _____

Paperwork _____

1. Practice.

Victor: Hello, Sara. Can you help me?
Sara: Sure. What do you need?
Victor: I have an application.
But how do I fill in the dates?
Sara: OK. What's your date of birth?
Victor: It's January 14, 1972.
Sara: Write 1/14/72 like this.
Victor: OK.
Sara: When did you come to the U.S.?
Victor: On December 5, 1990.
Do I put 12/5/90 on this line?
Sara: Yes. Now sign your name.
Don't print. And write today's date.

Date of birth: __1__ / __14__ / __72__

Date of entry to U.S.: __12__ / __5__ / __90__

Victor Honey
Signature

Date __2__ / __8__ / __92__

2. Fill in the form.

Date of birth: _____ / _____ / _____

Date of entry to U.S.: _____ / _____ / _____

_____
Signature

Date _____ / _____ / _____

3. Interview three classmates. Use a separate piece of paper.

What's today's date? _____

What's your date of birth? ____1/14/72_____

When did you come to the U.S.? ____12/5/90_____

Reading and Writing

1. **Vincent is a machine operator at C. J. Roberts and Company. What's wrong with his time sheet?**

C.J. Roberts and Company — Time Sheet

Employee's Name (please print) Vincent (Last)   Smith (First)

Job Title _____

Date	In	Out	In	Out	Total
31/3/92		8:00	12:00		4
1/4/92		8:00	12:00		4
2/4/92		8:00	12:00		4
3/4/92		8:00	12:00		4
4/4/92		8:00	12:00		4

Signature: Vincent Smith

Weekly Total 20

2. **Read Carrie's note to Vincent.**

> Vincent,
> Please put your last name first.
> Please fill in the blank with your job title.
> Write the month first, then the day.
> Don't write the day first.
> Put 8:00 in the "In" box.
> Put 12:00 in the "Out" box.
> Sign your name. Don't print.
> Thanks.
>
> Carrie

3. **Write a new time sheet for Vincent.**

C.J. Roberts and Company — Time Sheet

Employee's Name (please print) _____ (Last)   _____ (First)

Job Title _____

Date	In	Out	In	Out	Total

Signature:

Weekly Total

Reading and Writing

4. Read Carmen's story.

My name is Carmen Soto.
I'm from Mexico and my first language is Spanish.
I'm a widow.
I have two children, Albert and Marta.

I live in Bridgeton, California now.
I go to the Westside Community Adult School.
I study English in the morning.
My teacher's name is Sara Gilbert.

I work at C. J. Roberts and Company in the afternoon.
I'm a machine operator.
At night, I'm tired.

On Saturday, I clean my house and do the laundry.
On Saturday evening, I visit my friends.
On Sunday, my family comes over for dinner.
I'm happy.

**5. Write about yourself. Use a separate piece of paper.
Use Carmen's story as an example. Begin this way:**

My name is _____

I'm from _____ and my first language is _____

I'm _____

6. Read your story to your group.

Interactions

Student A

1. Get information. Ask about:

a. Han Fu's date of birth
b. May's Social Security number
c. Lily's date of birth
d. John's Social Security number
e. Han Fu's home phone number
f. Han Fu's work address

A: What's ___Han Fu's date of birth___ ?

B: ___March 25, 1944___ .

A: ___March 25, 1944___ ?

B: That's right.

GROUP HEALTH MEDICAL INSURANCE ENROLLMENT FORM

EMPLOYEE

Last Name	First Name	M.I.	Date of Birth
Chang	Han Fu	–	3/25/44

Marital Status: ☐ Single ☑ Married ☐ Separated ☐ Divorced ☐ Widowed

Street Address	Apartment
1555 Jefferson Street	–

City	State	ZIP Code
Bridgeton	California	93203

Telephone	Social Security Number	Occupation
	653-14-8017	cook

DEPENDENTS

Last Name	First Name	M.I.	Date of Birth	Social Security No.	Relationship
Chang	May	L.	12/28/46		wife
Chang	Lily	–		135-42-9540	daughter
Chang	John	M.	7/31/80		son

EMPLOYER

Name	Telephone
Good Luck Restaurant	(209) 565-1473

Street Address	

City	State	ZIP Code

Employee's Signature: _Han Fu Chang_ Date __2/8/92__

2. Give information.

Interactions

Student B

1. **Give information.**

   A: What's <u>Han Fu's date of birth</u>?

   B: <u>March 25, 1944</u>.

   A: <u>March 25, 1944</u>?

   B: That's right.

GROUP HEALTH MEDICAL INSURANCE ENROLLMENT FORM

EMPLOYEE

Last Name	First Name	M.I.	Date of Birth
Chang	Han Fu	–	3/25/44

Marital Status: ☐ Single ☑ Married ☐ Separated ☐ Divorced ☐ Widowed

Street Address _____ Apartment –

City _____ State _____ ZIP Code

Telephone (209) 593-8028	Social Security Number	Occupation cook

DEPENDENTS

Last Name	First Name	M.I.	Date of Birth	Social Security No.	Relationship
Chang	May	L.		706-25-8581	wife
Chang	Lily	–	8/16/76		daughter
Chang	John	M.		122-40-6119	son

EMPLOYER

Telephone _____

Name Good Luck Restaurant

Street Address 789 Fifth Avenue   ZIP Code 93205

City Bridgeton,   State California

Employee's Signature: *Han Fu Chang*   Date 2/8/92

2. **Get information. Ask about:**

   a. Han Fu's Social Security number
   b. May's date of birth
   c. Lily's Social Security number
   d. John's date of birth
   e. Han Fu's work phone number
   f. Han Fu's home address

Progress Checks

1. **a** ☐   Read and respond to warning signs.

   Who is right? Circle the picture.

2. **d** ☐   State your job.
     c ☐   Name some jobs.

   What are the people saying?

Do it yourself.

Progress Checks ✔

3. **g** ☐ Write dates.
    h ☐ Sign your name.

Fill in the form.

Employee's Name: _____ Date of Birth: __/__/__

Employee's Signature: _____ Date: _____

4. **b** ☐ Ask to use someone's things and respond.
    f ☐ Read dates.
    e ☐ Give dates.

What are the people saying?

Do it yourself. Read your partner's date of birth.

❧❧❧❧❧ MEMO ❧❧❧❧❧

TO: the teacher

Create an employment office. Students are job seekers, counselors, and actors in job demonstration "videos." List jobs on the board. Five or six groups of actors choose jobs to demonstrate. Job seekers watch each "video" in turn until they can guess the jobs being demonstrated. Then they tell a counselor which job they want. Counselors tally the choices, pool their numbers, and report to the class.

Grammar Summaries

Present Tense of *be*

I am	=	I'm			
we are	=	we're			
you are	=	you're			
they are	=	they're			
he is	=	he's			
she is	=	she's			
it is	=	it's			

I'm		
We're	(not)	from Peru.
You're		
They're		
He's		
She's		
It's		

Am	I	late?
Are	we you they	
Is	he she it	

Yes,	I	am.
	we you they	are.
	he she it	is.

No,	I'm	not.
	we're you're they're he's she's it's	

What	are	they?
Where	is	it?
Who		
How old		
How much		

Present Continuous Tense

I'm		
We're	(not)	working.
You're		
They're		
He's		
She's		
It's		

Am	I	working?
Are	you we they	
Is	he she it	

Yes,	I	am.
	we	are.
	he	is.

No,	I'm we're he's	not.

are not = aren't
is not = isn't

No,	we	aren't.
	he	isn't.

What	are	you	buying?
	is	he	

How	are	you	paying?
	is	he	

Simple Present Tense

I We You They	work
He She It	works.

do not = don't
does not = doesn't

I We You They	don't	work.
He She It	doesn't	

Do	I we you they	work?
Does	he she it	

Yes,	I	do.
	he	does.

No,	I	don't.
	he	doesn't.

Where When How	do	you	go?
	does	he	

Imperatives

Wait.	
Close	the door.
Open	your notebook.

	use the time clock.
Don't	go.

There is/There are

there is = there's

There's		a phone	on the corner.
There	are	phones	

Is	there	a phone	on the corner?
Are	there	phones	

Yes, there	is.
	are.

No, there	isn't.
	aren't.

Pro-Predicate *do*

What	are	you	doing?
	do	you	do?

Articles

a	phone robbery
an	operator emergency

Demonstratives

that is = that's

That's		my brother.
This	is	
Those	are	my brothers.
These		

Feel + Adjective

They	feel	sick.
She	feels	

Possessive Adjectives

(I)	my
(we)	our
(you)	your
(they)	their
(he)	his
(she)	her
(it)	its

That's	my	house.
	our	
	your	
	their	
	his	
	her	
	its	

Locations

It's	at	302 Ninth Avenue.
	on	Ninth Avenue.
		the shelf.
	in	Room 101.
	next to	
	between	the office and Room 101.

Time

It's	at	9:30.
	on	Friday.

Tapescript

UNIT 1   Page 5   Listening Plus.

Exercise 2. Point.

1. T T   F F   B B   G G
2. V V   J J   S S   D D
3. Y Y   E E   U U
4. A A   O O   I I

Exercise 4. Write the letters you hear.

1. A: What's your name?
   B: Carmen.
   A: How do you spell that?
   B: C-A-R-M-E-N.
   A: C-A-R-M-E-N?
   B: That's right.

2. A: What's your last name?
   B: It's Chang. C-H-A-N-G.
   A: Excuse me?
   B: Chang. C-H-A-N-G.
   A: Thanks.

3. A: How do you spell your name?
   B: N-E-A-R-Y.
   A: That's N-E-A-R-Y?
   B: That's right.

4. A: What's your friend's name?
   B: It's Yuki.
   A: Could you spell that?
   B: Sure. Y-U-K-I.
   A: Y-U-K-I?
   B: That's correct.

5. A: What's Carlos's last name?
   B: It's Gomez.
   A: I'm sorry. Could you repeat that?
   B: Gomez. G-O-M-E-Z.
   A: That's G-O-M-E-Z?
   B: Yes.
   A: Thanks.

6. A: What's your first name please?
   B: It's Marie.
   A: Excuse me?
   B: Marie. M-A-R-I-E.
   A: Is that M-A-R-I-E?
   B: Yes, that's right.

7. A: How do you spell your name?
   B: P-A-B-L-O.
   A: I'm sorry. Could you repeat that?
   B: Sure. It's P-A-B-L-O.
   A: Thank you.

8. A: What's your name?
   B: It's Babacar.
   A: Excuse me?
   B: Babacar. B-A-B-A-C-A-R.
   A: B-A-B-A-C-A-R?
   B: Yes, that's right.

UNIT 2   Page 17   Listening Plus.

Exercise 1. Point.

4 6 9 2 zero 5 8 10 7 3 1

Exercise 2. Point.

8 2 10 6 4 zero 5 3 1 9 7

Exercise 4. Fill in the area codes you hear.

a. A: Can I have the area code for Los Angeles?
   B: Certainly. That's two-one-three.
   A: Two-one-three?
   B: That's correct.

b. A: Do you know the area code for Washington, D.C.?
   B: Yes, it's two-oh-two.
   A: Can you repeat that, please?
   B: Two-oh-two.
   A: Thanks.

c. A: Do you remember the area code for Fort Worth?
   B: Uh-huh. It's eight-one-seven.
   A: Eight-one-seven?
   B: That's right.

d. A: Can I have the area code for Vancouver, British Columbia, please?
   B: One moment please. It's six-oh-four.
   A: Six-oh-four?
   B: That's correct.

e. A: What's the area code for Miami?
   B: Let me check. Here it is. Three-oh-five.
   A: Can you repeat that, please?
   B: Three-oh-five.

f. A: Could you tell me the area code for Gary, Indiana?
   B: Sure. Two-one-nine.
   A: Did you say two-one-nine?
   B: That's right.

Exercise 5. Fill in the phone numbers you hear.

a. A: What's your phone number?
   B: Three-two-six, three-five-eight-nine.
   A: Can you repeat that?
   B: It's three-two-six, three-five-eight-nine.
   A: Thanks.

b. A: I'm sorry. I don't remember your phone number.
   B: It's five-six-six, seven-eight-seven-one.
   A: Excuse me?
   B: Five-six-six, seven-eight-seven-one.
   A: Thanks.

c. A: What's Marie's phone number?
   B: Three-four-seven, nine-nine-six-six.
   A: Is that three-four-seven, nine-nine-six-six?
   B: That's right.

d. A: What's your phone number?
   B: Area code seven-one-three, eight-two-three, six-oh-two-nine.
   A: Could you repeat that?
   B: Sure. Area code seven-one-three, eight-two-three, six-oh-two-nine.
   A: Thank you.

e. A: His number is two-one-two, three-six-two, oh-one-oh-four.
   B: Two-one-two, three-six-two, oh-one-oh-four?
   A: Yes, that's right.

f. A: You can call me at area code three-one-two, six-nine-two, six-five-one-nine.
   B: Area code three-one-two...
   A: Six-nine-two, six-five-one-nine.

UNIT 3   Page 29   Listening Plus.

Exercise 1. Point.

A: 70.
B: 70?
A: Yeah. Seven-oh.

A: What's your apartment number?
B: It's 14.
A: 14?
B: Yes. One-four.

A: What floor are you on?
B: 13.
A: Which?
B: 13. That's one-three.

A: How much?
B: 80.
A: Sorry?
B: 80. Eight-oh.

A: I have 90.
B: How many do you have?
A: 90.
B: Is that nine-oh?
A: Yes.

A: How much?
B: 15.
A: I'm sorry?
B: 15. One-five.

Exercise 3. Point.

26 23 25 22 28 24 29 27 21

Exercise 4. Write the number you hear.

A: How old is she?
B: She's 22.
A: 22? She looks younger.

A: There are 52 cards.
B: How many?
A: 52.

A: My grandfather is 96 years old.
B: How old?
A: 96.
B: Wow! That's old.

A: My address is 77 Main Street.
B: What's the address?
A: 77 Main Street.
B: Thanks.

A: I have 65 cents.
B: Did you say 65?
A: Yes.

A: What's your room number?
B: 44.
A: What?
B: I'm in room 44.
A: Thanks.

UNIT 4 Page 41 Listening Plus

Exercise 1. Point.

400 800 200 900 1100 100 600
300 1000 700 500

Exercise 2. Point.

A: What's the address?
B: It's 100 Fourth Street.
A: 100 Fourth Street.
B: Yes. That's right.

A: What's your address?
B: It's 800 Seventh Street.
A: I'm sorry. Can you repeat that?
B: 800 Seventh Street.
A: Thanks.

A: Where do you live?
B: 1100 Fifth Street.
A: Where?
B: 1100 Fifth Street.

A: I live at 200 Eighth Avenue.
B: Could you please repeat that?
A: Yes. It's 200 Eighth Avenue.
B: Thanks.

A: Where does he live?
B: He lives at 5400 Second Avenue.
A: Excuse me?
B: 5400 Second Avenue.
A: OK. Thanks.

A: Where is the post office?
B: It's at 700 First Avenue.
A: 700 First Avenue?
B: Yes. That's right.

Exercise 3. Point.

a. A: What's the address?
    B: It's 438 Ninth Street.
    A: 438 Ninth Street?
    B: Yes. That's right.

b. A: What's your address?
    B: It's 1015 Eighth Street.
    A: I'm sorry. What's that?
    B: 1015 Eighth Street.
    A: Thanks.

c. A: Where do you live?
    B: 1328 Fifth Avenue.
    A: Excuse me?
    B: 1328 Fifth Avenue.

d. A: I live at 6212 First Street.
    B: Could you please repeat that?
    A: Yes. It's 6212 First Street.
    B: Thanks.

e. A: Where does he live?
    B: He lives at 576 Third Avenue.
    A: Could you repeat that for me?
    B: 576 Third Avenue.
    A: OK. Thanks.

f. A: Where is the hospital?
    B: It's at 59 Sixth Avenue.
    A: 59 Sixth Avenue?
    B: Yes. That's right.

Exercise 5. Write the numbers you hear.

a. A: Where do you live?
    B: At 67 Ninth Avenue.
    A: Where?
    B: At 67 Ninth Avenue.

b. A: My address is 7812 First Avenue.
    B: Is that 7812?
    A: Yes. That's correct.

c. A: What's the address?
    B: 1994 Main Street.
    A: I beg your pardon?
    B: 1994 Main Street.
    A: Thanks.

d. A: Do they have a new address?
    B: Yes. It's 4300 Broadway, second
       floor.
    A: 4300?
    B: Yeah. That's right.

e. A: Where does your mother live?
    B: She's at 9304 Second Avenue.
    A: Sorry?
    B: 9304 Second Avenue.
    A: Thanks.

f. A: Can you give me the address?
    B: Sure. 200 Ontario Avenue.
    A: 200? Thanks.

g. A: Where do you live?
    B: I'm at 7361 River Road.
    A: Excuse me?
    B: 7361 River Road.
    A: Thanks.

h. A: Please give me your address.
    B: OK. It's 900 Hill Street.
    A: 900?
    B: Yeah. You got it.

i. A: Where can I find the library?
    B: It's downtown at 2368 Front Street.
    A: Did you say 2368?
    B: Yes. On Front Street.

j. A: Where does Jim live?
    B: He lives at 825 Central Avenue.
    A: I'm sorry. I didn't get that.
    B: It's 825 Central Avenue.
    A: Thanks.

UNIT 5 Page 53 Listening Plus

Exercise 1. Point.

A: What's that?
B: It's a dime.
A: A what?
B: Ten cents. A dime.

A: How much money do you need?
B: Twenty dollars.
A: How much?
B: I told you. Twenty dollars.

A: Look! I found a penny!
B: Keep it. Finding a penny is good luck.
A: Oh. I didn't know that.

A: Is that money yours?
B: What money?
A: That ten-dollar bill on the table.
B: No. I didn't put ten dollars on the
   table.

A: What do you have in your hand?
B: A quarter.
A: What?
B: A quarter. Twenty-five cents.

A: How much is that book?
B: Not much. Only five dollars.
A: Excuse me. How much did you say?
B: I said it's only five dollars.

Exercise 2. Point.

A: How much is it?
B: It's two dollars and forty-nine cents.
A: How much?
B: Only two dollars and forty-nine cents.
   It's on sale.
A: Thanks.

A: What does it cost?
B: It's seventy-five cents.
A: Seventy-five cents?
B: Yeah, that's right.

A: How much do they cost?
B: They're four dollars.
A: I'm sorry. What was that?
B: Four dollars.
A: Oh. Thank you.

A: What's the price?
B: Seven dollars and forty-nine cents.
A: Only seven dollars and forty-nine cents? I'll take it.

A: Excuse me. How much is that chocolate bar?
B: It's fifty-five cents.
A: OK. I have fifty-five cents.
B: Here you go.

A: I want a nice gift for my husband. How much is this?
B: Twenty-four dollars and ninety-nine cents.
A: Twenty-four dollars and ninety-nine cents is a little expensive. Do you have anything else?

Exercise 3. Write the prices you hear.

a. A: What's the total?
   B: It's five dollars and fifty cents.
   A: Excuse me? How much?
   B: Five dollars and fifty cents.
b. A: What's the price?
   B: Thirty dollars.
   A: Did you say thirty dollars?
   B: Yes, I did.
   A: I'm sorry. Thirty dollars is just too much for me to spend right now.
c. A: How much for the batteries?
   B: Six dollars and twenty-nine cents.
   A: I beg your pardon?
   B: Six dollars and twenty-nine cents.
   A: Thanks.
d. A: What are you asking for this?
   B: It's nine dollars and eighty-nine cents.
   A: How much?
   B: Nine dollars and eighty-nine cents.
   A: Thank you.
e. A: What does this book cost?
   B: The price is on the back cover.
   A: Is it three dollars and ninety-five cents?
   B: That's correct. Three dollars and ninety-five cents.
f. A: Can you tell me the price of this shirt?
   B: Sure. That's eighteen dollars and seventy-five cents.
   A: It's pretty expensive.
   B: I don't think so. Eighteen dollars and seventy-five cents seems like a good price to me.
g. A: How much are the eggs?
   B: They're one dollar and forty-nine cents.
   A: How much?
   B: One dollar and forty-nine cents.

h. A: This is cute. How much is it?
   B: It's four dollars.
   A: Four dollars? I'll take it.

UNIT 6   Page 65   Listening Plus

Exercise 1. Point.

A: Where do you want the TV?
B: The TV? Oh, put it down anywhere.

A: I'm looking for the cat. Have you seen her?
B: Did you look under the bed?
A: Under the bed? Yes, that's the first place I looked.

A: Be careful! The stove is hot.
B: What did you say?
A: I just turned on the stove. It's hot.

A: Excuse me. How much is that lamp?
B: The blue or the black lamp?
A: The black one.
B: That's thirty-nine dollars and eighty-five cents.
A: Thank you.

A: Look over there. Someone broke that big mirror.
B: Poor guy.
A: Why do you say that?
B: Don't you know? It's bad luck to break a mirror.

A: I love that old chair.
B: Oh, really?
A: Yes, it was my grandfather's. Whenever I see that chair, I think of him.

Exercise 2. Write the word you hear.

a. A: Where are my books?
   B: Your books are on the bed.
   A: On the bed? Thanks.
b. A: Is the sofa new?
   B: No, that's my old sofa.
   A: It looks new.
   B: I cleaned it.
c. A: Hello. This is Pat Jones in Apartment 5H. My toilet isn't working.
   B: Excuse me? What did you say, Pat?
   A: The toilet isn't working in my apartment.
   B: OK. I'll be there in a minute.
d. A: Please put dinner on the table.
   B: Just a minute. Mike's working on the table.
   A: Ask him to put his things away, please. It's time for dinner.
e. A: The stove is broken.
   B: What do you mean?
   A: I mean I can't turn the stove on.
   B: OK. I'll fix it this afternoon.

f. A: Let's move the mirror out of the living room.
   B: OK. I'll move the mirror. Where do you want me to put it?
   A: Between the door and the window.
g. A: It's really dark in here.
   B: Yeah. I know. I could use another lamp.
   A: I have a lamp you can have.
   B: That would be great. Thanks.
h. A: Where are my keys?
   B: They're on your dresser.
   A: They're not on my dresser.
   B: Then look next to the phone.

Exercise 4.   Point.

A: Are you going to the kitchen?
B: To the kitchen? Yes. Why?
A: Could you get me a glass of water?
B: Sure.

A: I think there's someone in the living room.
B: In the living room? Are you sure?
A: Yes. I heard a noise.

A: What color are you going to paint the bathroom?
B: We haven't decided about the bathroom yet. Probably white or yellow.

A: I can't find my glasses.
B: Did you leave them in the bedroom again?
A: The bedroom. I bet that's where they are.

Exercise 5. Write the word you hear.

a. A: Where's Tom?
   B: He's in the living room.
   A: The living room? Thanks.
b. A: The window in the bathroom's broken.
   B: The bathroom window? Again?
   A: Yes. Can you believe it?
c. A: The sink in my kitchen isn't working.
   B: Your kitchen sink?
   A: Yes. Can you fix it?
   B: Sure. I'll be right up.
d. A: Where are you going?
   B: To the bedroom.
   A: The bedroom? Can you get my book for me, please?
   B: Sure.

UNIT 7   Page 77   Listening Plus

Exercise 1. Point.

A: What time is it?
B: Five thirty.
A: Excuse me?
B: Five thirty.

A: When does the train arrive?
B: The schedule says six forty-five.
A: And what does the arrival board say?
B: Six forty-five.

A: My first class begins at ten oh five.
B: That's funny. My first class begins at ten oh five, too.

A: I'm hungry. What time is it?
B: It's one o'clock.
A: One o'clock! No wonder I'm hungry.

Exercise 2. Point.

A: Excuse me. What time is it?
B: It's six forty.
A: Six forty? Thanks.

A: Do you have the time?
B: Yes. It's one ten.
A: One ten? I've got to hurry! I'm late!

A: Excuse me. When's the next bus to Bridgeton?
B: I think it's at three thirty-five.
A: Three thirty-five? Are you sure?
B: No, I'm sorry. I'm not.

A: What time does class end?
B: At twelve o'clock.
A: When?
B: Twelve o'clock.
A: Thanks.

A: When do you start work?
B: Five fifteen.
A: Five fifteen… Oh, you must be on the second shift.
B: That's right.

A: I have to be home at seven twenty.
B: Seven twenty? Why so early?
A: I promised to help my son with his homework.

A: What time does the movie start?
B: Well, there's a late afternoon show at four twenty-five.
A: Four twenty-five sounds great. Let's go.
B: Fine.

Exercise 4. Write the times you hear.

a. A: Excuse me. What time is it, please?
   B: It's eight fifteen.
   A: Eight fifteen? Thanks.

b. A: What time is it?
   B: It's two forty-five.
   A: I'm sorry. What did you say?
   B: Two forty-five.
   A: Thank you very much.

c. A: When do you usually wake up?
   B: I wake up at nine o'clock.
   A: Nine o'clock! Wow! You sleep late.

d. A: When do you want to meet for lunch?
   B: How about twelve thirty?
   A: Twelve thirty's fine with me.

e. A: When does the evening class begin?
   B: It starts at five fifteen.
   A: I'm at work at five fifteen. Is there a later class?

f. A: Do you have the time?
   B: Yes. It's one oh five.
   A: One oh five. Thank you very much.

g. A: When do you want to leave?
   B: How about seven o'clock?
   A: Seven in the morning? No way!

h. A: I need to speak with you. When can I make an appointment?
   B: I have time at four forty.
   A: OK. Four forty is good for me, too.
   B: Good. I'll see you then.

UNIT 8   Page 89   Listening Plus.

Exercise 1. Point.

A: Are you all right? Your nose is bright red.
B: My nose? Oh, that's nothing. Just a little paint.

A: Sorry I'm late. I had to see the doctor about my foot.
B: Your foot?
A: Yes. I hurt it running in the park last week.

A: Look how that man is holding that woman's hand.
B: He isn't holding her hand! He's trying to steal her purse! Stop him!

A: Why are you holding your stomach like that?
B: I don't feel very well. I have a little stomachache.
A: Oh, I'm sorry.
B: I'll be OK. I just ate too much at lunch.

A: What's wrong with your leg?
B: It's kind of sore. Someone kicked my leg instead of the soccer ball yesterday.

A: I have a toothache. Do you have any aspirin?
B: Sure, but if your tooth really hurts, you should go to the dentist.
A: I know I should. But I'm afraid of the dentist.

Exercise 4. Write the part of the body you hear.

a. A: I have a pain in my chest.
   B: Really? Are you OK?
   A: Don't worry about it. It's probably something I ate.

b. A: How do you feel?
   B: Terrible. I have a really bad headache.
   A: If your head hurts, you should take some aspirin.
   B: You're right. I think I will.

c. A: What's wrong with your ear, Tom?
   B: I don't know. I'm going to the doctor tomorrow to find out.

d. A: My back is killing me.
   B: Why don't you lie down and take it easy?
   A: I can't. I've got too much work to do.
   B: Well, be careful. Your back could get worse, you know.

e. A: Are you OK?
   B: Not really. I have a sore throat.
   A: My grandmother always says you should drink hot tea with honey and lemon for a sore throat.
   B: Sounds delicious. I think I'll try some.

f. A: Could you take a look? I think there's something in my eye.
   B: Which one?
   A: The right one.

g. A: What's the matter?
   B: Oh, I have a stiff neck today.
   A: Why don't you put ice on it?
   B: That's a good idea. I hadn't thought of that.

h. A: Did you know you have an earring on your right ear but not on your left ear?
   B: Oh, no. I must have lost it when I was shopping.

UNIT 9   Page 101   Listening Plus

Exercise 1. Point.

A: When's your father's birthday?
B: The 13th. October 13th.

A: What floor do you work on?
B: On the 18th.
A: Excuse me. What did you say?
B: The 18th floor.

A: Happy anniversary! Which one is it?
B: Our 40th.
A: Wow! Your 40th anniversary. That's a long time to be married.

A: What day are you taking off?
B: The 19th.
A: The what?
B: The 19th, Monday.

A: Does this bus go to 11th Street?
B: 11th? Yes, it does.

A: I love this movie. This is the 20th time I've seen it.
B: Did you say the 20th?
A: That's right.

Exercise 3. Point.

A: Where do Pat and Sue live?
B: On 25th Street.
A: Where?
B: On 25th, near the park.
A: Oh, I know where that is.

A: Happy birthday! Is it really your 29th?
B: My 29th birthday? Yes, as a matter of fact it is.

A: Sorry I'm late. I was waiting for the bus on 21st Street.
B: On 21st Street? There's no bus on 21st Street.
A: That's what I found out.

A: When's your last day of work?
B: Friday, the 24th.
A: The 24th? I didn't realize you were leaving so soon.

A: Do you know if this bus goes to 28th Avenue?
B: I think it goes to 28th, but I'm not sure. You'd better ask someone else.

Exercise 4. Write the number you hear.

a. A: Where do you live?
   B: On 65th Street.
   A: 65th Street. That's not far from where I live.
   B: Great. Maybe we can get together sometime.

b. A: Where do you go to school?
   B: On 86th Street.
   A: What school's on 86th Street?
   B: The Grand Avenue Adult Learning Center.
   A: Oh. That's right.

c. A: Where does your mother live?
   B: She lives on 17th Road.
   A: 17th. Is that near the high school?
   B: Yes, it's very near.

d. A: When's your birthday?
   B: September 29th.
   A: What a coincidence. My sister's birthday's September 29th, too.

e. A: What floor do you live on?
   B: The 43rd.
   A: The 43rd? And you're not afraid being so high up?
   B: No. Heights don't bother me.

f. A: Happy anniversary!
   B: Thanks. It's our 38th.
   A: Your 38th! Have you really been married that long?

g. A: Excuse me. Where's the train station?
   B: On 72nd Street.
   A: Is that East 72nd or West 72nd?
   B: East.
   A: Thank you.

h. A: I work on 94th Street.
   B: 94th. That's a long way from your house, isn't it?
   A: It sure is. It takes me an hour to get there.

i. A: When's the Halloween party?
   B: October 31st.
   A: Great. See you on the 31st.

Unit 10 Page 113 Listening Plus

Exercise 1. Point.

A: When's Valentine's Day?
B: February 14th.
A: February 14th? Are you sure?
B: Yeah. It's always the 14th.

A: Do you know when the first day of summer is?
B: I'm pretty sure it's June 21st.
A: I think you're right. June 21st sounds right to me.

A: When's your birthday?
B: August 22nd.
A: August 22nd. So you're a Virgo.

A: When do they celebrate the new year in your country?
B: The same day you do here—January 1st. Why?
A: Well, some countries don't have New Year's on January 1st.
B: Really? I didn't know that.

A: When's American Independence Day?
B: July 4th.
A: Oh, that's right. The Fourth of July.

A: When's St. Patrick's Day?
B: It's always on March 17th.
A: I'm sorry. When is it?
B: March 17th.
A: Thanks.

Exercise 3. Point.

A: When did Columbus reach the New World?
B: In 1492.
A: That's right. 1492.

A: This music is great. What's it called?
B: It's the 1812 Overture.
A: Oh, yeah. The war of 1812. The music sounds like a war.

A: When did the United States declare independence from Britain?
B: In 1776.
A: Only 200 years ago?
B: Yes. July 4th, 1776.

A: What year was Mike born?
B: In 1959.
A: Did you say 1959?
B: Uh-huh.

A: When was this movie made?
B: In 1984.
A: Are you sure?
B: Yes. It says here, 1984.

Exercise 4. Write the date you hear.

a. A: When was your mother born?
   B: On October 18th, 1932.
   A: October what?
   B: October 18th, 1932.

b. A: When did get your green card?
   B: July 22nd, 1991.
   A: I'm sorry. I couldn't hear.
   B: I said July 22nd, 1991.

c. A: When did you come to the United States?
   B: On December 8th, 1990.
   A: December 8th?
   B: 1990.

d. A: When did you and Hector get married?
   B: April 15th, 1978.
   A: In 1978, on April 15th.

e. A: What's your date of birth?
   B: June 1st, 1958.
   A: I beg your pardon?
   B: It's June 1st, 1958.

f. A: When did you start your first job?
   B: A long time ago. September 18th, 1947.
   A: September 18th, 1947. That was a long time ago!
   B: I know it is, but it doesn't feel like it.

g. A: When was your daughter born?
   B: On January 22nd, 1956.
   A: When?
   B: January 22nd, 1956.

h. A: When did you graduate?
   B: May 12th, 1975.
   A: Excuse me?
   B: May 12th, 1975.

Basic Conversations

for Progress Checks: *What are the people saying?*

UNIT 1

2. A: What's your first name?
   B: Rosa.
   A: How do you spell that?
   B: R-O-S-A.
   A: What's your last name?
   B: Gomez.
   A: How do you spell that?
   B: G-O-M-E-Z.

3. A: Close the door.
   B: *(Closes the door.)*

   A: Point to the clock.
   B: *(Points to the clock.)*

   A: Open the book.
   B: *(Opens the book.)*

4. A: Hi. I'm Mary./My name is Mary.
   B: Hi, Mary. I'm Sara./My name is Sara.
   A: Mary, this is Ann.
      Ann, this is Mary.
   C: Nice to meet you.
   B: Nice to meet you.
      Where are you from?
   C: I'm from China.

UNIT 2

2. A: What's your area code?
   B: 917.
   A: What's your phone number?
   B: 555-1324.
   A: Can you repeat that?
   B: 555-1324.

3. A: Hi, Ed. How are you?
   B: Fine, thanks. How are you?
   A: Fine, thanks.

4. A: Who's that?
   B: That's my son.
   A: What's his name?
   B: His name is Victor.

UNIT 3

2. A: Who's your teacher?
   B: Alba Sanchez.
   A: What level are you in?
   B: Level 2.
   A: What's your room number?
   B: 27.
   A: What's your first language?
   B: It's Spanish.
   A: How old are you?
   B: 45.
   A: 45?
   B: Yes.

3. A: Where are the books?
   B: They're on the shelf.
   C: Where's the men's room?
   B: It's next to the office.

UNIT 4

2. A: What's your address?
   B: 415 West Street.
      Bridgeton, California.
      93205.

3. A: 911. What's the emergency?
   B: An accident.
   A: Where?
   B: On West Street between First Avenue and Second Avenue.

4. A: Where's the library?
   B: On the corner of West Street and Ninth Avenue.

UNIT 5

2. A: Where's the aspirin?
   B: Aisle 3.

3. A: How much are the razor blades?
   B: $3.95.
   A: What's the total?
   B: $55.68.

UNIT 6

1. A: Who is it?
   B: It's Ms. Davidson.
   A: The sink isn't working.

3. A: Hello.
   B: Hello. This is John Burgos.
      Can I speak to Paula?
   A: I'm sorry. She's not here.
   B: Thanks.

UNIT 7

2. A: What time is it?
   B: It's 3:05.

3. A: Do you work on Saturday?
   B: No, I don't. I work on Sunday.

4. A: Do you want to go to the movies on Thursday?
   B: I'm sorry. I'm busy on Thursday.
   A: How about Friday?/Are you free on Friday?
   B: Friday is fine.

UNIT 8

2. A: What's your marital status?
   B: I'm married.

3. A: What's the matter?
   B: My back hurts./I have a backache.

5. A: Thank you.
   B: You're welcome.
   A: Goodbye./Bye.
   B: Goodbye.

UNIT 9

1. A: Where do you live?
   B: On West Street between Fourth Avenue and Fifth Avenue.
   A: Where's that?
   B: Near Community Hospital.

2. A: Where does this bus go?
   B: Union Park.
   A: I'm going to West Hospital.
      Where do I get off?
   B: Get off at West Street.

3. A: How do I get to Ann's house?
   B: Go one block.
      Turn left.
      Go one block.

      OR

      Go one block on C Street.
      Turn left on 6th Road.
      Go straight to B Street.
      It's on the corner.

UNIT 10

2. A: What do you do?
   B: I'm a teacher.
   A: He's a mechanic.

4. A: Can I use your eraser?
   B: Sure. *(Gives eraser to A.)*
   A: *(Points to own date of birth.)*
   B: *(Reads date aloud.)* May 21, 1965.